The New York Times

CHANGING PERSPECTIVES

War

T0282814

EDUCATIONAL PUBLISHING
BOOKS

THE NEW YORK TIMES EDITORIAL STAFF

Published in 2019 by New York Times Educational Publishing
in association with The Rosen Publishing Group, Inc.
29 East 21st Street, New York, NY 10010

First Edition

The New York Times
Alex Ward: Editorial Director, Book Development
Brenda Hutchings: Senior Photo Editor/Art Buyer
Phyllis Collazo: Photo Rights/Permissions Editor
Heidi Giovine: Administrative Manager

Rosen Publishing
Greg Tucker: Creative Director
Brian Garvey: Art Director
Megan Kellerman: Managing Editor
Julia Bosson: Editor

Cataloging-in-Publication Data
Names: New York Times Company.
Title: War / edited by the New York Times editorial staff.
Description: New York : The New York Times Educational Publish-
ing, 2019. | Series: Changing perspectives | Includes glossary and
index.
Identifiers: ISBN 9781642820676 (pbk.) | ISBN 9781642820669
(library bound) | ISBN 9781542820652 (ebook)
Subjects: LCSH: War—Juvenile literature. | Terrorism—Juvenile
literature. | Conflict management—Juvenile literature. | Fighting
(Psychology—Juvenile literature.
Classification: LCC U21.2 W37 2019 | DDC 303.6'25--dc23

Manufactured in the United States of America

On the cover: Iraqi Special Operations Forces soldiers survey the
aftermath of an ISIS suicide car bomb that managed to reach their
lines in the Al Andalus neighborhood of East Mosul; Ivor Prickett
for The New York Times.

Contents

CHAPTER 3

The Vietnam War

CHAPTER 4

The Iraq War

CHAPTER 5

The War on Terror

Introduction

ON THE MORNING of September 11, 2001, terrorists hijacked two commercial airplanes and flew them into the towers of the World Trade Center. Another plane was flown into the Pentagon, and a fourth crashed in a field in Pennsylvania after passengers led a revolt. Less than a week after these attacks, the most severe terrorist incident in American history, President George W. Bush declared a war on terror. What followed was more than a decade of military engagement in Afghanistan, Iraq, Yemen, and Pakistan. Overnight, America became a nation at war. Again.

The articles in this book are arranged around five of the major conflicts America has been involved in over the last century: World War I, World War II, the Vietnam War, the Iraq war, and the war on terror. Each war began from a confluence of different forces; each concluded with a different notion of "victory." But for those at home, a primary way to follow the progression of a battle and keep track of their loved ones was from the pages of newspapers and reporting of journalists like those at The New York Times.

War correspondents put their lives at risk. In search of facts, journalists report alongside soldiers on the frontlines of the battlefield. Some of their pieces, like the 1916 report from Verdun, France, evoke the experience of being at war. Other reporters describe commanders' perspectives, as in the piece on President Obama's choice to deploy more troops to Afghanistan. And some reporting investigates and challenges the very premise of the war being fought. For example, the Times's reporting on the Pentagon Papers in 1971 exposed the government's deception in matters relating to Vietnam, undermining the justification for America's involvement in the conflict itself.

A statue of Saddam Hussein in front of the burning National Olympic Committee in Baghdad in 2003.

By the very nature of war, facts are hard to come by and each side has a vested interest in controlling the narrative. For this reason, unbiased, independent journalism is essential in times of conflict. Many of the articles in this book were written contemporaneously with the events being reported. Others were written retrospectively. Looking at the two in conjunction, it is evident that often the facts on the ground change faster than the reporting can keep up with. Some events that appeared to be historic were overwritten by unforeseen developments just hours later. Decisions deemed necessary at the time years later appear foolhardy, even criminal. From primary reporting to later pieces informed by thorough, historical research, the articles in this collection demonstrate the ways in which our understanding of a given conflict can be as malleable as the events themselves.

Throughout these pieces run a series of philosophical questions: Is war necessary? Can it be justified? Who loses what in times of conflict? Ultimately, the United States is more experienced at war than peace. From the Revolutionary War, to the Civil War, to the war on terror, wars have been essential to the establishment of an American nation and a patriotic identity. It may just be a fact of existence.

CHAPTER 1

World War I

The First World War began in 1914 when Archduke Franz
Ferdinand of Austria was assassinated on the streets of
Sarajevo by a group of Serbian nationalists. What followed
were four years of grueling, bloody hostilities that entan-
gled almost three dozen countries. Fought in trenches
across Europe, in international waters by warships and
U-boats, and on three different continents, the war
became known as the War to End All Wars. Its resolution,
however, paved the way for another major international
conflict just twenty years later.

All the Powers Massing Great Armies in Fear of Possible Conflict.

BY THE NEW YORK TIMES | JULY 30, 1914

LONDON, THURSDAY, JULY 30 — Premier Asquith's simple announcement
to the House of Commons yesterday that the European situation,
growing out of the Austro-Russian crisis, was one of extreme gravity,
summarizes the present position of affairs.

The exchange of views that was proceeding between the Russian Foreign Minister, Sazonoff, and the Austro-Hungarian Ambassador in St. Petersburg, Szapáry, have ceased. On the other hand,
German diplomacy is believed to be trying to re-establish relations
between St. Petersburg and Vienna. The result of these efforts is
not known.

An exchange of telegrams is alleged to have taken place between
the German and Russian Emperors.

Rumors of an impending mobilization of the German Army are circulating in several Continental capitals, but these rumors are not yet confirmed.

The hostilities between Austria and Serbia, which, according to one report, have resulted in setting Belgrade afire, shrink into insignificance before the military preparations which are reported to be in progress in every part of Europe. In most countries these are described as precautionary measures, but they are upon a scale never before known in history.

The news of Russia's partial mobilization, given in the St. Petersburg dispatch to The New York Times yesterday, is confirmed. In diplomatic circles Russia is understood to have informed Germany that only the southern and southwestern corps of the Russian Army are mobilizing. These sixteen corps at their war strength represent 1,200,000 men. In the event of war the Czar, it is stated, will take the field as the Commander in Chief.

The Russian mobilization, according to St. Petersburg, affects only the Austrian, not the German frontier, and does not imply war between Russia and Austria.

SAYS RUSSIA SPOILED PEACE PARLEYS

The Frankfurter Zeitung, whose Berlin telegrams are frequently inspired, asserts that the Russian mobilization has prejudiced the diplomatic negotiations "perhaps fatally."

According to The London Times this morning, direct diplomatic intercourse between Austria-Hungary and Russia was suspended yesterday. This suspension indicates the growing tension of the situation. Since October, 1908, when diplomatic intercourse was interrupted between Russia and Austria-Hungary after the annexation by the latter of Bosnia and Herzegovina, there have been several periods of such silence.

In the Spring of 1909 and again in the Winter of 1912-13 large bodies of Russian and Austro-Hungarian troops faced each other for months on either side of the Russo-Galician frontier. On the latter occasion the ominous silence between Vienna and St. Petersburg was broken only by the action of Emperor Francis Joseph in dispatching Prince Gottfried von Hohenlohe-Langenburg to the Russian Court on a special mission.

The gravity of the present situation lies less in the breaking off of the exchange of views than in the fact that the breach followed upon the Austro-Hungarian declaration of war against Serbia.

BRITISH FLEET LEAVES PORTLAND

Great Britain's first fleet, under the command of Admiral Sir George A. Callagan, left Portland yesterday morning under sealed orders, amid stirring scenes. A large number of officers and men who were ashore on leave were called out from theatres and moving picture-palaces the previous evening, the announcements being made from the stage that every man had to be aboard by 10 o'clock. The excited audiences rose as the men left and cheered heartily, while the orchestras played "Rule, Britannia."

Thousands of persons congregated about the pier where the Jack Tars arrived arm in arm with their sweethearts. Women in evening dress were driven to the pier in taxicabs to bid their husbands and sweethearts goodbye.

An Admiralty note of warning has been circulated throughout the British fleet and all naval stations ashore. All the officers and men are especially cautioned against communicating any information to the press or to unauthorized persons. It is pointed out that great mischief may result from apparently unimportant items of information becoming public.

Voice of Verdun: France's Reply to Peace Hints

BY G. H. PERRIS | DEC. 18, 1916

VERDUN, FRIDAY, DEC. 15 (DISPATCH TO THE LONDON DAILY CHRONICLE) — In the great battle of Verdun, where the French Army struck another deadly blow at the forces still nominally commanded by the German Crown Prince, on the Heights of the Meuse. In a few hours the Germans were beaten back an average of two miles on a six and a half mile front. Many thousands of prisoners were taken and a number of cannon captured or destroyed. As a high officer said to me this afternoon, and there was no boasting accent in his voice: "All our objectives are attained."

I was able to watch the whole operation, as well as actions of such an extent can be watched, from 10 o'clock this morning, when the French infantry climbed over the parapets, till nightfall, when it only remained to hold what had been won. From the French positions of this morning, except Douaumont, the highest point of the plateau, the Meuse Heights rise tier beyond tier.

From a certain happily situated hill most of the battlefield was clearly visible, and every considerable movement could be closely followed. Heavy purple clouds filled the sky, but only a few scurries of rain and sleet fell during the day, and the dark hillsides rising toward the central crest of Douaumont remained clear of mist. This was an important advantage, for the French aviators were able to carry on without cessation their valuable work, despite a strong and icy wind. Great biplanes and little Nieuports came and went, while a dozen "sausages" held permanent guard at the end of their long cables. There must have been some German planes near the front, but I did not see one on the French side of the lines, and I only saw one German observation balloon, and that was falling like a huge torch beyond Douaumont, an incident typical of the Germans' day.

GUNS SILENT FOR A MOMENT.

Just before 10 o'clock there was a hush in the cannonade, a momentary pause in which we knew hundreds of officers were following the second hands of their watches and thousands of men were standing ready for the signal with bayonets fixed and bags of bombs adjusted, and to complete the heavy load the only food and drink they could hope to receive for many hours. Modern assaults go by clock work, at least the minute timing of the advance is the basis upon which the added information of aviators, rocket signallers and telephonists is superimposed.

When, therefore, the given moment arrived. It was rather like a spontaneous movement of a vast mechanism than a noisy and confused clash of old-time armies. Suddenly the hills echoed with the multitudinous flapping and crashing of hundreds of hidden guns. The green and brown slopes and the valley of the amphitheatre were fuller of gun flashes than the frosty sky is with stars.

The other end of the trajectory of the French barrage fire was visible in long lines of the smoke of exploding shells preceding with marvelous closeness the advancing lines of blue-coated Infantry. The French three-inch field gun was always famous for its rapidity and exactitude, and a tactic has gradually been evolved which exploits these qualities to the fullest. Occasional accidents are inevitable, but they are nothing in the poilu's mind now that he realizes the advantage of advancing behind a moving wall of flame. Everywhere the sky flashed with the rising and falling flames of signal rockets, and in every part of the front intrepid airmen swim in and out of the zone of death. Wonderful and terrible is this panorama, with its narrow fringe of smoke in front and its mysterious thousands of spitting flames behind. More learned observers remarked that after the beginning of the attack the German artillery fire became erratic and ineffectual, probably from fear that the near guns would he captured, as most of them were.

I now pass to a more detailed review of the advance, starting from the left or west wing in the Meuse Valley. Here the village of Vacherauville, lying between the long ridges of Talou and Poivre, had been fortified in the now familiar manner, being linked up with the latter by a strong trench running right up to the hill. Grenade fighting continued for several hours on the villages, and it was not until the commanding positions on the east had been lost that its last defenders gave in and the capture of Pepper (Poivre) Hill was speedily accomplished. The Germans had a triple system of trenches along the slope up to the summit, marked 342 metres, and on the south side of the road from Vacherauville to Louvemont. These had been much shattered, and the whole crest was cleared by bombing parties with uncanny rapidity under the protection of the French curtain fire.

MANY OF VICTORS COLONIALS.

This great victory is the work of four French divisions, including many of the colonial troops who captured Douaumont last month. They started from points reached in their earlier advance. It completely alters the balance of advantageous positions on the Meuse Heights. Yesterday, although they no longer held the two highest summits, Douaumont and Souville, the Germans had abundant observatories and long views down ravines running southward in the centre of the plateau. In losing these hills and perspectives they lose all control over the central mass of this mountain, and another push equal to that of today would put them back to the line they occupied before Fcb. 21 last.

Snow began to fall as I left the field last evening, and is falling more heavily today. Much of the conquered ground is a foul bog in which for the moment trenches cannot be dug, and General Winter is a more redoubtable foe than any Boche. The heroism of holding such ground when the evacuation of the wounded is made horribly difficult, and the bringing up of every pound of bread and every pint of water is titanic labor, appears to me more conspicuous than that by which it was seized.

The Germans received a very heavy blow. Among 8,000 or 9,000 prisoners made in the last twenty-four hours there are between 200 and 300 officers. The time when German officers generally died fighting has passed. As to the men, there is a good deal of evidence that they now stand in open fear of the French. There are strong elements among them, but they are not numerous enough to sustain the weak stuff that has been mixed with them. The decline of their morale is marked. Their organization is still formidable, but it develops no new resources or quality to meet the increase of the material strength of the Allies — the Allies' superiority in practically every specialist service and tactical science in which the French are first masters.

In recent actions on the Meuse, the Germans have tended to revert to the earlier practice of holding the foremost trenches in strength, perhaps because thinly held lines could not be trusted to resist at all. The only result so far has been to increase their losses of all kinds.

FRENCH LOSSES SLIGHT.

As on the last occasion when Douaumont was recovered, the French casualties are relatively small owing to the successful barrages, the speed of the advance and the disorganization of the German batteries. All the characteristics of a clean victory are therefore seen in this affair, inferior losses and positions taken of great tactical importance for a future heavy blow at the German morale. This last quality is enough enhanced by the circumstances of the moment.

The battle of Louvemont, as we may call it from its central position, brings back the true proportion and perspective to our interpretations of the map of war. The Kaiser and his Chancellor have been answered by statesmen, and will be answered by diplomatists, but I doubt whether any reply to their peace proposals will count for appropriateness and emphasis besides the thunderous voice of Verdun, for Verdun, which speaks not in words but only in immortal deeds, has become a sort of personality. The voice of Verdun is the invincible will of all France in its most deliberate expression. It means that this people is resolved not to be conquered and not to be tricked; it means that this people is conscious of its wounds, conscious of the weakness of alliances, conscious that the common foe has yet some serious remains of his original strength. The people are still more conscious of their own superiority on the battlefield. It is a clarion challenging a wearied foe, but I read also in that fierce voice the challenge no less to friends and partners than to the foes of France.

Wilson Approves Staff's Army Bill

BY THE NEW YORK TIMES | APRIL 7, 1917

WASHINGTON, APRIL 6 — President Wilson issued a statement today supporting in every detail the General Staffs plan for raising an army of a million men in a year, and adding further increments when needed. The President's statement is as follows:

"The principles embodied in the legislation presented by the War Department to the Military Committees of the Senate and House have my entire approval, and its specific recommendations embody the best Judgment of the officers of the War Department. It proposes to raise the forces necessary to meet the present emergency by bringing the regular army and the National Guard to war strength and by adding the additional forces which will now be needed, so that the national army will comprise three elements, the regular army, the National Guard, and the so-called additional forces, of which a first 500,000 are to be authorized immediately, and later increments of the same size as they may be needed.

"In order that all those forces may compose a single army, the term of enlistment in the three is equalized, and will be for the period of the emergency. The necessary men will be secured for the regular army and the National Guard by volunteering, as at present, until, in the judgment of the President, a resort to a selective draft is desirable. The additional forces, however, are to be raised by selective draft from men ranging in age from 19 to 25 years. The quotas of the several States in all of these forces will be in proportion to their population.

"This legislation makes no attempt to solve the question of a permanent military policy for the country, chiefly for the reason that in these anxious and disordered times a clear view cannot be had either of our permanent military necessities or of the best mode of organising a proper military peace establishment. The hope of the world is that when the European war is over, arrangements will have been made composing many of the questions which have hitherto seemed to require the arming of the nations, and that in some ordered and just way the peace of the world may be maintained by such cooperations of force among the great nations as may be necessary to maintain peace and freedom throughout the world.

"When these arrangements for a permanent peace are made, we can determine our military needs and adapt our course of military preparation to the genius of a world organized for justice and democracy. The present bill, therefore, is adapted to the present situation, but it is drawn upon such lines as will enable us to continue its policy, or so much of it as may be determined to be wise, when the present crisis has passed."

AWAIT ACTION BY CONGRESS.

In the War Department further moves award mustering a great army await action by Congress. Every preliminary step already has been taken, however, to carry out the project of raising and training 1,000,000 men in a year and supplying them with full war equipment.

News that the war status had been proclaimed by President Wilson was flashed to army and navy posts and ships throughout the world as soon as the war resolution was signed at the White House. The only other thing that can be done at the War Department without Congressional action is to order the regular army expanded to full war strength.

Plans have been laid for calling the full strength of the General Staff to Washington to help in administration of the huge task of army building before the department. Only half of the authorized strength of the staff can now be on duty here under existing law. Congress is expected to remedy this at once, however. Pending a decision by Congress on the methods to be employed in raising the army, a detailed scheme for appointment of new general officers and getting highly efficient soldiers in command of each regiment cannot be worked out. The basis for this work, however, already has been established by staff action.

Wide latitude has been left to the president in the selection of Generals under the staff plan. They may be appointed from any part of the forces to be raised or from civil life. Up to and including the grade of Colonel, however, is desired by the military officials that men who have had recent experience in handling troops shall be selected. So far as possible it is proposed to select regular army officers of experience to head all new regiments.

With thirty-two infantry and four cavalry divisions to be organized, there would be at least thirty-six Major Generals and three times that number of brigadiers to be selected and commissioned, with Colonels and Majors in proportion. The grade of Major is the highest provided for reserve officers, and that of Captain for the provisional list of enlisted men.

SIXTEEN TRAINING CENTRES.

The creation of sixteen training centres would provide for two infantry divisions at each post. Presumably, the centres for the four cavalry divisions would be somewhere in the region of the Mexican border, so that this mounted force could take over the border patrol work to a large extent, relieving the majority of the 60,000 regulars now assembled there.

With the calling out of the first 500,000 of the new army, provision would be made for a new division at each training centre, the forces already there supplying the instructors and all other machinery of organization, so that the half million young men could be absorbed into the army structure with little disorder or delay.

No further steps toward calling out the National Guard will be taken until Congress has acted. It is proposed to draft the entire guard into the Federal service, divorcing it from its militia status at once, instead of summoning them under their dual allegiance organizations. This can be done only with authority of Congress. When that has been granted, even the 60,000 guardsmen now in the Federal service on police duty will be drafted formally so as to do away with any possibility of dual authority over them or restriction on their use.

German Counter-Artillery Fire Silenced by Our Guns in 38 Minutes

BY CAMERON MACKENZIE | SEPT. 13 1918

SEPT. 12 (MORNING) — Early this morning the First American Army, assisted by certain French units, but all under the direct command of General Pershing, launched between the Moselle and the Meuse an attack with limited objectives upon a front of between thirty and thirty-seven miles.

The operation, which has for its purpose the wiping out of the St. Mihiel salient, eclipses in magnitude and importance all previous efforts of Pershing's troops in France and indubitably signalizes an entirely new phase in America's participation in the war.

It is much too early yet to give any details of the fighting proper. However, we have experienced a night of artillery preparation on a grand scale. It was at precisely 1 o'clock that the American guns unlimbered, and not since Verdun has the Valley of the Meuse known such a roar and rumble. Except close to the lines, there were not many flares against the sky, for the Autumn mists blanketed the flashes.

To one on the scene, however, the great thought is that the American army has passed from its initial stage and has become a distinct and separate military entity, going forth to do battle on its own account. It is a proud day for the young new army from overseas, and there was not an American boy who went pressing on to the inferno of shellfire who did not accept his ordeal with a little mere gallantry and a little more stoicism for the knowledge that at last his country was in the war "on its own."

SWEPT OVER SECOND LINE OF DEFENSES.

NOON — In my dispatch sent earlier today it was possible to do little more than record the fact that the American Army was engaged upon its first really large-sized independent operation in the war, and that it had taken upon itself the by no means simple task of pinching out the famous, well-fortified St. Mihiel salient, with its deep dip down between the Meuse and Moselle.

Although the details of the battle still in progress unfold themselves slowly, it is now possible, despite the lack of a general vision of the course of the entire engagement, to supply some additional information concerning the fighting.

Along a line which may he roughly described as running Southwest from Pont-a-Mousson the American troops have made progress. More than half a dozen villages have passed into their hands. The resistance encountered at the first system of German defenses, without being tame, was not actually stiff, and the doughboys were able to sweep toward the second line of enemy positions ahead of their schedule.

There, however, the Germans interposed a more definite negative to the advance, and encounters of the sharpest sort began to develop. This delayed, but in no wise daunted the Americans, who valorously pushed on northward.

That these operations have proceeded so successfully augurs well for a general success.

Southward from St. Mihiel two actions which are described as strong raids have taken place. AIso at several points along the heights of the Meuse the French troops have been exerting heavy pressure.

At the moment nothing presents itself with greater emphasis than the skill with which the American artillery fire was conducted. Not only did it achieve the most savage and devastating intensity, but was altogether remarkable for its accuracy. There must be that in the American character which lends itself to good gunnery.

When, fifteen minutes after the American fire had begun, the Germans' attempted to make a silencing retort, it took our artillerymen precisely thirty-five minutes to blot out the enemy's counterfire; and the suppression of counterfire is the supreme test of marksmanship in modern war.

At first the flashes did not partake at all of the character of heat lightning, which they so often do, but seemed wellnigh completely lost in the air. In the darkness only the streamers of signal rockets, insistently rising, managed to penetrate with any brilliancy the overspreading murkiness, but as the hours passed the misty rain abated, leaving a horizon of perfect black to serve as background, and to hold the flares in a continuously trembling blanket of light. Finally came day and it all paled to nothingness, save only the consciousness that below as far as the eye could reach the American lads were going grimly forward in their crusader's task.

It is hardly to be presumed that further stress need be laid upon that for which the St. Mihiel salient stands. Next to Ypres it may be said to be the most famous salient on the western front.

So far, to those following the American operation, the one great spectacle has been the night of shellfire which we have just experienced. From a hillside commanding a portion of the battle scene one's every sense was, at the exact turn of 1 o'clock this morning, most ruthlessly assaulted. Upon the instant those valleys, exquisitely soft and winsome, which the Meuse and the Moselle confine, became horrifying thunderpits.

One thought no longer of the chill of the trickling Autumn rain that was falling. Nearby guns surcharged the air with concussion waves that vibrated the muscles, and distant guns, when they were at all distinguishable in the general commotion of the right, seemed more than anything else merely to grunt.

Should America Have Entered World War I?

OPINION | BY MICHAEL KAZIN | APRIL 6, 2007

ONE HUNDRED YEARS ago today, Congress voted to enter what was then the largest and bloodiest war in history. Four days earlier, President Woodrow Wilson had sought to unite a sharply divided populace with a stirring claim that the nation "is privileged to spend her blood and her might for the principles that gave her birth and happiness and the peace which she has treasured." The war lasted only another year and a half, but in that time, an astounding 117,000 American soldiers were killed and 202,000 wounded.

Still, most Americans know little about why the United States fought in World War I, or why it mattered. The "Great War" that tore apart Europe and the Middle East and took the lives of over 17 million people worldwide lacks the high drama and moral gravity of the Civil War and World War II, in which the very survival of the nation seemed at stake.

World War I is less easy to explain. America intervened nearly three years after it began, and the "doughboys," as our troops were called, engaged in serious combat for only a few months. More Americans in uniform died away from the battlefield — thousands from the Spanish flu — than with weapons in hand. After victory was achieved, Wilson's audacious hope of making a peace that would advance democracy and national self-determination blew up in his face when the Senate refused to ratify the treaty he had signed at the Palace of Versailles.

But attention should be paid. America's decision to join the Allies was a turning point in world history. It altered the fortunes of the war and the course of the 20th century — and not necessarily for the better. Its entry most likely foreclosed the possibility of a negotiated peace among belligerent powers that were exhausted from years mired in trench warfare.

Although the American Expeditionary Force did not engage in combat for long, the looming threat of several million fresh troops led German generals to launch a last, desperate series of offensives. When that campaign collapsed, Germany's defeat was inevitable.

How would the war have ended if America had not intervened? The carnage might have continued for another year or two until citizens in the warring nations, who were already protesting the endless sacrifices required, forced their leaders to reach a settlement. If the Allies, led by France and Britain, had not won a total victory, there would have been no punitive peace treaty like that completed at Versailles, no stab-in-the-back allegations by resentful Germans, and thus no rise, much less triumph, of Hitler and the Nazis. The next world war, with its 50 million deaths, would probably not have occurred.

The foes of militarism in the United States had tried to prevent such horrors. Since the war began, feminists and socialists had worked closely with progressive members of Congress from the agrarian South and the urban Midwest to keep America out. They mounted street demonstrations, attracted prominent leaders from the labor and suffrage movements, and ran antiwar candidates for local and federal office. They also gained the support of Henry Ford, who chartered a ship full of activists who crossed the Atlantic to plead with the heads of neutral nations to broker a peace settlement.

They may even have had a majority of Americans on their side. In the final weeks before Congress declared war, anti-militarists demanded a national referendum on the question, confident voters would recoil from fighting and paying the bills so that one group of European powers could vanquish another.

Once the United States did enter the fray, Wilson, with the aid of the courts, prosecuted opponents of the war who refused to fall in line. Under the Espionage and Sedition Acts, thousands were arrested for such "crimes" as giving speeches against the draft and calling the Army "a God damned legalized murder machine."

The intervention led to big changes in America, as well as the world. It began the creation of a political order most citizens now take for granted, even as some protest against it: a state equipped to fight war after war abroad while keeping a close watch on allegedly subversive activities at home.

The identity of the nation's enemies has changed often over the past century. But at least until Donald Trump took office, the larger aim of American foreign policy under both liberal and conservative presidents had remained much the same: to make the world "safe for democracy," as our leaders define it. To achieve that purpose required another innovation of World War I: a military-industrial establishment funded, then partly and now completely, by income taxes.

For all that, the war is largely forgotten in the United States. Combatants in World War II and Vietnam are memorialized in popular sites on the National Mall, but the men who fought and died in the Great War have no such honor (though there is a small memorial specific to soldiers from Washington, and a small national monument is in the planning stages).

Alone among the former belligerent nations, the United States observes a holiday on the anniversary of the Armistice — Veterans Day — that makes no explicit reference to the conflict itself. The centennial of the declaration of war is a good time to remember how much the decision to enter it mattered.

MICHAEL KAZIN IS THE AUTHOR OF "WAR AGAINST WAR: THE AMERICAN FIGHT FOR PEACE, 1914-1918," A PROFESSOR OF HISTORY AT GEORGETOWN AND THE EDITOR OF DISSENT.

Long Echoes of War and Speech

OPINION | BY TED WIDMER | AUGUST 13, 2014

WOODROW WILSON is almost never quoted by name when modern presidents speak, but he remains audible all the same, particularly in the echoes that still reverberate a hundred years after the Great War.

In late May, President Obama spoke at West Point, where he defined America's place in the world much as Wilson might have — propping up the international order, defending human rights, and walking eternally down the path of virtue. George W. Bush, so different in so many ways, also radiated Wilsonian idealism, even as he claimed to be an un-Wilsonian realist. His second Inaugural Address, drawn straight from the Wilson playbook, declared "the ultimate goal of ending tyranny in our world." That remains a work in progress.

Wilson did not speak this way when World War I broke out in the summer of 1914. At first, he barely mentioned the diplomatic catastrophe unleashed by the assassinations at Sarajevo. On July 27, the day before Austria declared war on Serbia, he gave a press conference, and said meekly, "The United States has never attempted to interfere in European affairs." Wilson's silence coincided with a personal crisis of his own. His wife Ellen lay dying that summer, and when one of his daughters asked him about the growing chance of war, he said simply, "I can think of nothing — nothing, when my dear one is suffering." She expired on Aug. 6, as the war began.

But his silence also reflected astonishment that war was breaking out, against all expectations, in an era that had at least as many clichés about globalization as our own. And it stemmed from an old presidential tradition, soon to be shattered, of avoiding grandiose statements about human betterment. George Washington, in his Farewell Address, specifically urged Americans to steer clear of foreign conflicts. The Monroe Doctrine proposed noninterference by Americans in Europe, as well as the opposite. Theodore Roosevelt advocated for silence as well — his famous adage to speak softly and carry a big stick — even if he did not always achieve it.

Wilson showed no signs of breaking from this tradition, at first. After Sarajevo, he gave a Fourth of July address that never even mentioned the killings a week earlier. Americans seemed to approve. In 1916, "He Kept Us Out of War" was a popular slogan that helped Wilson to eke out victory over his Republican rival, Charles Evans Hughes.

But Wilson's silence would eventually give way to a different voice, the one that we remember him for. In the spring of 1917, after three horrific years, the world had changed greatly, and so had he. As he brought the United States to the precipice of war, he began to speak in a way that has defined the American presidency ever since. It was not merely that the United States would enter a European theater for the first time, in huge numbers. Wilson also asked that Americans fight to make the world "safe for democracy." In a sense, he asked the United States to become the world's judge as well as its sheriff, with an evangelical optimism that has brought both inspiration and exasperation to the 96 percent of the world that is not American.

Earlier presidents had expressed some of these aspirations: Thomas Jefferson proclaimed America the "world's best hope" in his first inaugural, and Lincoln had often expressed himself likewise, in a language of aspiration. But these remarks expressed only a forlorn wish. They never formed a policy aim, and they fell far short of calling for intervention in Europe, where violations of human rights were as easy to find as the next hillside.

By 1917, Wilson was ready to take that step. He was hardly a natural interventionist. But the war was increasingly affecting American noncombatants, and insulting human rights on an epic scale, with mounting civilian casualties, chemical weapons, and the targeting of neutral vessels.

Accordingly, in the spring of 1917, Wilson began to deliver a stream of public statements that broke his earlier silence, and defined war not so much as a military exercise as an attempt to set the world right.

Suddenly, a new language of human rights was being delivered by a president, from something like a pulpit, backed for the first time with the full might of American power.

On Feb. 26, he asked Congress to declare "armed neutrality," a precursor to war, to defend the world's "fundamental human rights." His second inaugural, on March 5, promised to fight for "the principles of a liberated mankind." In his war message of April 2, Wilson announced that a new age had begun, in which Americans would make the world safe, not only for democracy, but a broad catalog of rights that included freedom of the seas, the independence of small nations, and the right of all nations to unite, to "make the world itself at last free."

That was a tall order. But since then, we have never stopped marching toward a goal that remains a bit otherworldly. Wilson was an effective messenger in 1917, drawing on his Presbyterianism, his grasp of American history, and his childhood memory of growing up in a region that had recently been occupied by an invading army (inconveniently, that of the United States). In this sense, Wilson's language of self-determination might be understood as a final legacy of the Civil War.

The language of 1917 proved durable. Without doubt, Franklin D. Roosevelt's messages during World War II were improved by his articulation of the core freedoms Americans were fighting for. The better speeches of the Cold War — John F. Kennedy's in particular — conveyed a vivid sense of what American values meant to the world. Yet a tone of high moral dudgeon could also weaken a presidential speech, when it proved ineffective, or untethered to economic reality, or borderline delusional — Lyndon Johnson's insistence that democracy was coming soon to Vietnam, or George W. Bush's similar predictions for Iraq.

It has become fashionable to criticize Wilson for naïveté as well as self-righteousness. Evangelical statements require some suspension of disbelief, but ultimately, as he learned the hard way, soaring aspirations have a way of crashing back to earth. American forces did join the battle in 1917, and they tipped the balance, giving thrust to Wilson's promises. But democracy, that catch-all term, proved difficult when he returned home from his European peacemaking efforts in 1919 and tried to enlist a skeptical Congress behind his vision of an improved world order. At the same time, the words linger, expressive of something elusive that presidents still seek to articulate. As it turned out, a prophecy he made in his Fourth of July speech in 1914 was self-fulfilling: "The most patriotic man, ladies and gentlemen, is sometimes the man who goes in the direction that he thinks right even when he sees half the world against him." A century later, that is often what American foreign policy feels like, as we reel from one undemocratic place to another, hoping to limit the carnage. To aspire to the best in Wilson's oratory, while guarding against the worst, feels like a reliable course for a nation still finding its way in a world that has yet to be made safe for anything.

TED WIDMER IS ASSISTANT TO THE PRESIDENT FOR SPECIAL PROJECTS AT BROWN UNIVERSITY. HE RECENTLY EDITED "LISTENING IN: THE SECRET WHITE HOUSE RECORDINGS OF JOHN F. KENNEDY."

The War to End All Wars? Hardly. But It Did Change Them Forever.

BY STEVEN ERLANGER | JUNE 26, 2014

ZONNEBEKE, BELGIUM — To walk the orderly rows of headstones in the elegant graveyards that hold the dead of World War I is to feel both awe and distance. With the death of the last veterans, World War I, which began 100 years ago, has moved from memory to history. But its resonance has not faded — on land and geography, people and nations, and on the causes and consequences of modern war.

The memorial here at Tyne Cot, near Ypres and the muddy killing ground of Passchendaele, is the largest British Commonwealth cemetery in the world. Nearly 12,000 soldiers are buried here — some 8,400 of them identified only as "A Soldier of the Great War, Known Unto God." Despite the immensity of this space, the soldiers represent only a tiny portion of the 8.5 million or more from both sides who died, and that number a fraction of the 20 million who were severely wounded.

In Europe's first total war, called the Great War until the second one came along, seven million civilians also died.

Yet the establishment of these grave sites and monuments, here and in villages all over the Western Front, is more than a reminder of the scale of the killing. World War I also began a tradition of memorializing ordinary soldiers by name and burying them alongside their officers, a posthumous recognition of the individual after the trauma of mass slaughter.

World War I could be said to have begun in Sarajevo on June 28, 1914, with the assassination of Archduke Franz Ferdinand and his wife, Sophie, by a young nationalist seeking a greater Serbia. The four and a half years that followed, as the war spread throughout Europe, the Middle East and Asia, reshaped the modern world in fundamental ways.

The war destroyed kings, kaisers, czars and sultans; it demolished empires; it introduced chemical weapons, tanks and airborne bombing;

A field gun in a small forest known as Belleau Wood, where, with Germans positioned in shallow trenches or firing from inside a stone hunting lodge, the United States Marines kept assaulting until the battle was finally won.

it brought millions of women into the work force, hastening their legal right to vote. It gave independence to nations like Ukraine, Poland and the Baltic countries and created new nations in the Middle East with often arbitrary borders; it brought about major cultural changes, including a new understanding of the psychology of war, of "shell shock" and post-traumatic stress.

It also featured the initial step of the United States as a global power. President Woodrow Wilson ultimately failed in his ambitions for a new world order and a credible League of Nations, setting off much chaos with his insistence on an armistice and his support for undefined "self-determination." And the rapid retreat of the United States from Europe helped sow the ground for World War II.

Historians still squabble over responsibility for the war. Some continue to blame Germany and others depict a system of rivalries, alliances and anxieties, driven by concerns about the growing weakness of the Austro-Hungarian and Ottoman Empires and the growing strength of Germany and Russia that was likely to produce a war in any case, even if there was some other casus belli.

But the emotional legacies are different for different countries. For France the war, however bloody, was a necessary response to invasion. Preventing the German Army from reaching Paris in the first battle of the Marne spelled the difference between freedom and slavery. The second battle of the Marne, with the help at last of American soldiers, was the beginning of the end for the Germans. This was France's "good war," while World War II was an embarrassing collapse, with significant collaboration.

For Germany, which had invested heavily in the machinery of war, it was an almost incomprehensible defeat, laying the groundwork for revolution, revanchism, fascism and genocide. Oddly enough, says Max Hastings, a war historian, Germany could have dominated Europe in 20 years economically if only it had not gone to war.

"The supreme irony of 1914 is how many of the rulers of Europe grossly overestimated military power and grossly underestimated economic power," Mr. Hastings said, a point he now emphasizes when speaking with Chinese generals. The Germans, too, are still coming to terms with their past, unsure how much to press their current economic and political strength in Europe.

For Britain, there remains a debate about whether the British even had to fight. But fight they did, with millions of volunteers until the dead were mounded so high that conscription was finally imposed in 1916. The memory of July 1, 1916, the first day of the Battle of the Somme — when 20,000 British soldiers died, 40,000 were wounded and 60 percent of officers were killed — has marked British consciousness and become a byword for mindless slaughter.

"The sense that the war was futile and unnecessary still hangs over a lot of the discussion in Britain," said Lawrence Freedman, professor of war studies at King's College, London.

In Britain there is also a deep presumption that the generals were incompetent and cold to human sacrifice, that "lions" — the brave ordinary Tommies — were "led by donkeys" like Field Marshal Douglas Haig.

"That was almost certainly true at the start, but not true at the end," Mr. Freedman said. "But the notion that lives were lost on an industrial scale because generals kept trying to launch offensives for a few feet of ground is widespread."

In fact, the beginning of the war was mobile and extremely bloody, as were the last few months, when the big offensives of 1918 broke the German Army. The rate of killing in the muck and mud of the trenches was much lower than during the mobile part of the war.

If the inheritance is mixed, the war still casts a long shadow, refracted through what can now seem the inevitability of World War II and our tumultuous modern history. This is also, after all, the 75th anniversary of the start of that war and the 25th anniversary of the collapse of the Berlin Wall.

The end of the Cold War was in a sense a return to the end of World War I, restoring sovereignty to the countries of Eastern Europe, one reason they are so eager to defend it now.

Analysts wonder if the period of American and European supremacy itself is fading, given the rise of China and the return of traditional nationalism, not just in Russia but in the many euroskeptic voters in France, Britain and Denmark.

Inevitably, analogies are drawn. Some analysts compare Germany after the war to Russia now, arguing that just as Germany rejected the "Carthaginian peace" at the end of World War I, so Russia is now rejecting the "settlement" of the Cold War, seeing it as unjust, chafing over its defeat and prompting a new Russian aggressiveness and irredentism.

Some question whether the lessons of 1914 or of 1939 are more valid today. Do we heed only the lessons of 1939, when restraint was costly, and miss the lessons of 1914, when restraint could have avoided the war?

Trenches in the hills of Verdun. There were an estimated 550,000 French casualties and 434,000 German casualties during the battle, a third of which were fatalities.

Some see a continuing struggle between Germany and Russia for mastery of Europe, a struggle that marked both world wars and continues today, and not just in Ukraine, where a century ago its people fought on both sides. Others see World War I, at least as it began in Sarajevo, as the third Balkan War, while the post-Cold War collapse of Yugoslavia and its multinational, multicultural, multireligious model continues to present unresolved difficulties for Europe, in Bosnia, Kosovo and beyond. Similar tensions persist in Northern Ireland, the rump of Ireland's incomplete revolution that began with the Easter Rising of 1916.

Others point to the dangers of declining powers faced with rising ones, considering both China and the Middle East, where the Syrian civil war and the advance of Islamic militants toward Baghdad are ripping up the colonial borders drawn up in the Sykes-Picot agreement by the French and British, with Russian agreement, in 1916, the middle of the war, when the Ottoman Empire was cracking. The carnage at Gallipoli helped shape the national identity of the inheritor state, modern Turkey, let alone Australia.

Even the Balfour Declaration, which threw British support behind the establishment of a Jewish state in Palestine, was signed during the war, in November 1917.

With the new interest in the centenary, mourners and tourists, schoolchildren and relatives, walk the living battlefields of Ypres, which still turn up human remains and live ammunition. And they walk the finely kept grass between the gray headstones here at Tyne Cot, laying bright red poppies upon the earth.

The poppy is one of the most obvious inheritances of the Great War — made famous in the 1915 poem by a Canadian military doctor, Lt. Col. John McCrae: "In Flanders fields, the poppies blow, between the crosses row on row, that mark our place..." The short poem was written as a eulogy and a call to solidarity from the dead to the living, that they not "break faith with us who die."

Not far away is the tiny Flanders Field American Cemetery and Memorial, an exquisitely kept six acres containing only 368 graves, including 21 unknown, while the names of 43 more, missing in action, are carved on the walls of a small chapel.

If Tyne Cot is the largest military cemetery for the Commonwealth, this is the smallest American military cemetery. The headstones tell the stories of first- and second-generation Americans, their names redolent of the Europe their parents left to make a better life, who returned here to die. Like Giuseppe Spano, a private from Pennsylvania, and Angelo Mazzarella, a private from West Virginia, and Emil P. Wiser, a private from Montana, and Ole Olson, a private from Wisconsin, and John Dziurzynski, a private first class from Ohio.

"The dead were and are not," the historian G. M. Trevelyan wrote in his autobiography. "Their place knows them no more and is ours today. Yet they were once as real as we, and we shall tomorrow be shadows like them."

CHAPTER 2

World War II

In 1939, Hitler's army invaded Poland and, for the second time in a quarter-century, the world was plunged into bloody conflict. While the British, French, and Russian troops fought the Nazis in Europe, the United States engaged the Japanese in the East. The war officially came to an end in 1945 after Hitler's armies were forced into retreat and the United States dropped the first atomic bombs on Japan. At the end of the war, tens of millions of people were dead and the allied forces emerged as the world's new leaders.

The International Situation

BY THE NEW YORK TIMES | SEPT. 8, 1940

WITH A FURY not heretofore unleashed, German bombers attacked London last night. Censorship hid the exact extent of the damage, but official British admissions said it was great. Buildings in the heart of the city shook as if from an earthquake as the swastika-marked planes rained down tons of bombs and the overnight alarm of eight hours and eighteen minutes was the longest of the war. The British said the Germans had lost sixty-five planes in the attacks, which began in late afternoon, against eighteen of their own.

Berlin asserted that the attack on London had been carried out by the strongest air fleet ever concentrated on a single objective, numbering between 1,500 and 2,000 planes. They said that the assault was in retaliation for British night attacks on "non-military objectives" and that 2,200 tons of bombs had been dropped, leaving one single cloud of smoke from the center of London to the mouth of the Thames. The Nazis put the day's score of planes shot down at eighty-seven for the British and twenty-six of their own.

Reporting on Friday night's spectacular raid on Berlin, the British Air Ministry said that a power station, oil supplies and railroad yards had been successfully attacked. Other objectives on the night's list were industrial plants in the Ruhr and Rhine areas and airdromes and big gun emplacements along the German-held French Channel coast. The Germans said they intercepted a new raid last night, their antiaircraft and fighter defenses turning off R. A. F. bombers before they reached Berlin.

Fifty Iron Guardists were reported in Bucharest to have fired on the special train carrying former King Carol to temporary sanctuary in Switzerland. The report said they were attempting to halt the train to remove Magda Lupescu, whom they believed aboard, and were not trying to kill their former sovereign. The attack was made in Rumanian territory as the train neared the Yugoslav border. Bucharest had quieted down under the rule of General Ion Antonescu, who formed a new Cabinet in which he holds four posts and assumed the title of "Chief of State."

In France's temporary capital at Vichy it was revealed that two former Premiers, Edouard Daladier and Paul Reynaud, and the one-time Allied generalissimo, General Maurice Gustave Gamelin, were under "preventive arrest" in a chateau near Riom awaiting the war-guilt trials.

It was also revealed in Vichy that Herschel Grynszpan, the young Polish Jew whose assassination of a German diplomat in Paris touched off the November, 1938, attacks on the Jews in Germany, had been turned over to the Gestapo by French authorities and had been taken to Germany by auto. His fate was not revealed.

AMERICAN DEVELOPMENTS

The Burke-Wadsworth Selective Service Bill was passed last night by the House by a vote of 263 to 149. The Fish amendment, which would delay operation of the draft for sixty days, and another amendment, less harsh than that of the Senate, providing for government control and operation on a rental basis of plants whose owners refused to cooperate in the defense program, were accepted just before final passage. The bill now goes to conference for adjustment of differing Senate and House provisions.

The United States has informed its twenty sister American republics that the air and naval bases leased from Britain are for their use also, Secretary Hull revealed. The arrangement, it was expected, would he reciprocal, with the use of air and naval bases in those countries granted to the United States if that should become necessary for the common defense. Confirmation of a proposed sale of three over-age destroyers to Uruguay still was lacking, but the deal was believed to be in process of negotiation.

Differences between the National Defense Advisory Commission and the Treasury over amortization features of the Excess Profits Tax Bill brought a halt to the Senate Finance Committee's work of liberalizing and simplifying the bill's features so as to speed private defense plant construction.

War of the World: Japanese Attack Merges Conflicts — We Must Not Discount Foe's Strength

BY HANSON W. BALDWIN | DEC. 8, 1941

BOMBERS WITH THE Rising Sun flag of Japan painted upon their black wings flew over Pearl Harbor, "key to the Pacific," shortly after dawn yesterday and thus merged the Chinese war and the European war into a war of the world.

The crash of exploding bombs in the Hawaiian Islands, Guam and possibly the Philippines, the roar of anti-aircraft guns and the twisted, flaming skeletons of wrecked planes heralded the war of the Pacific, with the principal antagonists the United States and Japan — a war that has been long brewing, a conflict often predicted but previously avoided. But the Japanese aggression yesterday did more than start a Pacific war. It broadened the conflicts already raging into a world-wide struggle whose end no man can know.

The Japanese blows were struck — as had long been anticipated — without a declaration of war and without warning. But the temporary advantages the Japanese may have thus gained are more than offset by the psychological effect that the manner of their attack has had upon the United States. In the long view, those attacks were perhaps the most stupid action the Japanese could have taken, and were clearly by-products of the military mentality that has so long been a power-ful influence in Japan. For it is possible that the Japanese could have moved into Thailand without actual United States military interven-tion; few Americans wanted to "die for Thailand." But for the United States is another matter. The country is now unified and is girding itself for the first time with full strength for a struggle that will be hard and long, but which eventually must result in disaster for Japan.

EFFECTS ARE UNPREDICTABLE

The Japanese intervention in the war is certain to have far-reaching and unpredictable effects upon the struggle in Europe and upon the Battle of the Atlantic. For the democratic gains of the past few months — the upset of the German "timetable" in Russia, the recent Nazi reverse at Rostov, the assumption by the British of the offensive in North Africa, the marked reduction in ship sinkings — are now to some extent neutralized and countered by the entrance of Japan into a "shooting war" on the side of the Axis.

One factor, the strength of Japan, cannot and must not be discounted. There has been a distinct tendency in this country to underestimate Japanese military, naval and air forces; now that the final struggle has been joined, the nation must face the prospect of war with an opponent that possesses considerable strength — material as well as intangible strength — an opponent whose soldiers have one great attribute: they are not afraid to die. Our nation's slogan should be Churchillian in its inspiration — "blood, sweat and tears."

Some of this Japanese strength was evident in the treacherously sudden attacks yesterday that seemed — from the sparse information available — skillfully planned. The reports from the Philippines were conflicting and confusing, but it was evident that the heaviest Japanese blows were directed at Pearl Harbor, principal base of our Pacific fleet, on the island of Oahu, Hawaii.

The Japanese bombers and torpedo planes struck at ships moored in the narrow harbor there, and raked Ford Island in the center of Pearl Harbor, site of the Navy's patrol plane base. Hickam Field, the Army's great airfield near the entrance to Pearl Harbor, was also bombed. It is likely, however, that most of the planes at both fields were either in the air or based elsewhere when the attacks occurred.

Almost simultaneous attacks took place on virtually undefended Guam, and it is likely that other of our mid-Pacific outposts, perhaps Wake, Midway and Johnston Islands, were also bombed. At the same time sinkings, almost certainly attributable to Japanese submarines, were reported in the Eastern Pacific, and Japanese troops apparently have attacked Thailand.

PREMEDITATION INDICATED

All of this quite clearly indicates a premeditated plan on Japan's part, a plan that must have been launched with the departure of the men-of-war from Japanese ports at least a week — perhaps two weeks — ago.

The Japanese attacks apparently had one end in view — to strike at and weaken as quickly as possible the naval strength of her principal antagonist, the United States, before our superior strength could institute an effective war of attrition by long-range blockade and long-range bombardment. Singapore is the southern "anchor," Pearl Harbor the northern base, for the great ring of any such blockade; Japan chose to strike, apparently, at her strongest opponent first — knowing that if our Pacific Fleet could be materially damaged, or its base operations blocked or partially destroyed, weaker salients of our strength, such as the Philippines could be reduced later.

This war that has just been joined is a war of great distances, a war in which navies and air forces will at least initially play the major roles. Our navy today is probably the largest in the world, but it is divided between two oceans, and the British establishment of an Eastern fleet at Singapore does not wholly compensate for the transfers in the past month of some of our vessels to the Atlantic, for the vast distance between Pearl Harbor and Singapore results in a somewhat risky dispersion of strength.

FLEET IS THIRD LARGEST

The Japanese fleet is the world's third largest; it probably consists today of eleven capital ships (one of them new), with another nearly ready; eight or nine aircraft carriers, plus three carriers converted from merchantmen; forty-four to forty-six cruisers (seven of them obsolete, about five others of special types, fast mine-layers, etc.);

about 126 destroyers and sixty- nine or seventy submarines, some of them large craft of long range probably now operating in the Eastern Pacific.

The Japanese aviation, divided between the army and the navy (with the navy generally conducting over-water operations and all long-range overland raids) is believed to number between 3,000 and 5,000 combat planes with one recent estimate putting the total at 220 squadrons.

The Japanese Army at full mobilization consists of about sixty to sixty-six divisions (1,800,000 men), with perhaps twenty divisions or more in China, twenty to twenty-seven in Manchukuo, others in metropolitan Japan and in Formosa, Hainan, Indo-China and moving toward Thailand.

For Those Who Died

BY THE NEW YORK TIMES | MAY 7, 1945

IF THE JUBILATION over the collapse of one German army after another is less ecstatic than many had been anticipating, the reasons are not difficult to define. In the first place, we have another war of equal magnitude to win in the Far East. In the second place, we have won nothing in Germany that we have not paid for dearly. During the long uphill battle since the Nazis started to overrun the world, millions of men of many nations have fallen in strange places. Those who have died at sea and on the battlefields deserve nothing less than the defeat of Germany's military power and the destruction of Nazi despotism. What we have accomplished is the least we can do for the dead, the wounded, the hungry and the homeless who for nearly six years have trailed the bitter furrow plowed by the Nazi military machine. It is a tearful victory. We cannot celebrate it without remembering the dead.

Since wars are destructive, it is impossible to take much satisfaction in them. Many of us know from personal experience what they cost; we humbly hope that there may never be another. But we can take this much satisfaction in the destruction of Nazi Germany: everyone has known what he was doing. Thanks to Hitler's demoniac candor, every man has understood that he was fighting to preserve the freedom of nations. We may also take satisfaction in this magnificent proof that democracies, where public discipline is so chaotic, are invincible once they have been aroused, and that citizen armies and civilian industries can overwhelm neurotic militarism.

When the Nazi armies defeated France in the first shattering year of the war, Hitler's elation was recorded in his uncontrollable little dance caught in a motion picture. Overwhelming France seemed to be conquest for him. He could not make his arms and legs stay still. The success of our counter-offensive leaves us with no feeling of conquest. In a long, grinding offensive we have demonstrated that our faith in national freedom has not been misplaced. To our men this has been a hard job that had to be done, and they have done it. And to those men, fighting so far away from home, in a spirit of devotion to their families and country, we owe a debt that the San Francisco Conference may pay if men of good-will continue to stand together.

Enemy Maneuvers

BY THE NEW YORK TIMES | MAY 7, 1945

THE DAY OF victory in Europe is dawning with an Allied military triumph that is complete and overwhelming. A few formalities of Germany's surrender remain to be completed; a few doomed fanatics bent on selling their evil lives as dearly as possible must still be rooted out. But with the surrender of most of their armies, the Germans themselves have acknowledged defeat, and the American capture of the Skoda Works at Pilsen deprives even the die-hards of their last means to continue the struggle. Barring a few last-minute mopping-up operations, the European war is over, and formal announcement of V-E Day may be expected at any time.

The day of victory marks the end of a struggle which at one time threatened to overwhelm our civilization, and which in any case must leave deep moral and material scars for generations. But it also marks new beginnings. It marks the beginning of a new effort, now being made at San Francisco, to shape a better world in which such conflicts shall be made impossible. It also marks the beginning, first, of Germany's inevitable attempt to prepare for her comeback, as she did after the last war, and second, of Japan's equally inevitable political maneuvers to escape defeat. All these efforts depend upon each other. If San Francisco succeeds, the hopes of our enemies will be greatly dimmed. If San Francisco fails, our enemies still have a chance to rob us of the fruits of victory. And the key to the success or failure of these efforts is unity among the United Nations, and especially among Russia, Britain and the United States.

For the efforts of both Germany and Japan are now determined wholly by the hope that they may still succeed in what they failed to accomplish during the war in Europe—namely, in driving a wedge between the western Allies on the one hand and Russia on the other. Hitler, who as late as April 19 still predicted a break between the Allies "within two months," and on that basis urged continuation of the war to gain time so that he could join the "party which approaches me first — it makes no difference which," did not live to see his prophecy come true. But his successors are obviously following the same tactics — and the same hope.

They still proclaim that "resistance against the Soviets continues to save as many Germans as possible from Bolshevik terror"; they still seek to surrender to the western Allies alone, excluding Russia; and they have begun to falsify the unconditional surrender of their armies in the field into an "armistice" motivated, not by their defeat, but by the pretense that "the war against the western Powers has become senseless." In other words, faced with complete collapse, they still seek to propagate the legend that they fought to the last "to save Europe from Bolshevism," and that they went down only because once again they were "stabbed in the back" — this time not by "democratic traitors" at home, but by the "treachery" of the western democracies as a whole.

Seeking the same end, though by just the opposite route, Foreign Minister Togo declares from Tokyo that in asking for a separate peace with the western Allies, while continuing the war against Russia, Germany has violated the German-Japanese alliance, and that her action does not comport with the avowed war aims of Japan, which "is at war with the Anglo-American nations, but is strictly bound in neutrality with the Soviet Union." For that reason, Togo says, Japan reserves to herself the right "to act freely," which in itself is not only tantamount to an abrogation of the alliance with Germany, and the even older Anti-Comintern pact, both of which have lost their meaning, but also represents a first overture to Russia, which may soon he followed by others.

All these maneuvers have heretofore been defeated by the unbreakable military solidarity of the United Nations, demonstrated anew by the refusal of the British and American Governments and their field commanders to accept a German surrender that did not include Russia. But the end of military operations is bringing to the fore political problems of peace in the handling of which the western Allies and Russia must still find a common language — as demonstrated in the crucial case of Poland. Until they do, their common enemies will continue their efforts to split them, to the detriment of that new world which they are trying to create.

First Atomic Bomb Dropped on Japan; Missile Is Equal to 20,000 Tons of TNT; Truman Warns Foe of a 'Rain of Ruin'

BY SIDNEY SHALETT | AUGUST 6, 1945

WASHINGTON, AUG. 6 — The White House and War Department announced today that an atomic bomb, possessing more power than 20,000 tons of TNT, a destructive force equal to the load of 2,000 B-29's and more than 2,000 times the blast power of what previously was the world's most devastating bomb, had been dropped on Japan.

The announcement, first given to the world in utmost solemnity by President Truman, made it plain that one of the scientific landmarks of the century had been passed, and that the "age of atomic energy," which can be a tremendous force for the advancement of civilization as well as for destruction, was at hand.

At 10:45 o'clock this morning, a statement by the President was issued at the White House that sixteen hours earlier — about the time that citizens on the Eastern seaboard were sitting down to their Sunday suppers — an American plane had dropped the single atomic bomb on the Japanese city of Hiroshima, an important army center.

JAPANESE SOLEMNLY WARNED

What happened at Hiroshima is not yet known. The War Department said it "as yet was unable to make an accurate report" because "an impenetrable cloud of dust and smoke" masked the target area from reconnaissance planes. The Secretary of War will release the story "as soon as accurate details of the results of the bombing become available."

But in a statement vividly describing the results of the first test of the atomic bomb in New Mexico, the War Department told how an immense steel tower had been "vaporized" by the tremendous explosion, how a 40,000-foot cloud rushed into the sky, and two observers were knocked down at a point 10,000 yards away. And President Truman solemnly warned:

"It was to spare the Japanese people from utter destruction that the ultimatum of July 26 was issued at Potsdam. Their leaders promptly rejected that ultimatum. If they do not now accept our terms, they may expect a rain of ruin from the air the like of which has never been seen on this earth."

MOST CLOSELY GUARDED SECRET

The President referred to the joint statement issued by the heads of the American, British and Chinese Governments, in which terms of surrender were outlined to the Japanese and warning given that rejection would mean complete destruction of Japan's power to make war.

[The atomic bomb weighs about 400 pounds and is capable of utterly destroying a town, a representative of the British Ministry of Aircraft Production said in London, the United Press reported.]

What is this terrible new weapon, which the War Department also calls the "Cosmic Bomb"? It is the harnessing of the energy of the atom, which is the basic power of the universe. As President Truman said, "The force from which the sun draws its power has been loosed against those who brought war to the Far East."

"Atomic fission" — in other words, the scientists' long-held dream of splitting the atom — is the secret of the atomic bomb. Uranium, a rare, heavy metallic element, which is radioactive and akin to radium, is the source essential to its production. Secretary of War Henry L. Stimson, in a statement closely following that of the President, promised that "steps have been taken, and continue to be taken, to assure us of adequate supplies of this mineral."

The imagination-sweeping experiment in harnessing the power of the atom has been the most closely guarded secret of the war. America to date has spent nearly $2,000,000,000 in advancing its research. Since 1939, American, British and Canadian scientists have worked on it. The experiments have been conducted in the United States, both for reasons of achieving concentrated efficiency and for security; the consequences of having the material fall into the hands of the enemy, in case Great Britain should have been successfully invaded, were too awful for the Allies to risk.

All along, it has been a race with the enemy. Ironically enough, Germany started the experiments, but we finished them. Germany made the mistake of expelling, because she was a "non-Aryan," a woman scientist who held one of the keys to the mystery, and she made her knowledge available to those who brought it to the United States. Germany never quite mastered the riddle, and the United States, Secretary Stimson declared, is "convinced that Japan will not be in a position to use an atomic bomb in this war."

A SOBERING AWARENESS OF POWER

Not the slightest spirit of braggadocio is discernable either in the wording of the official announcements or in the mien of the officials who gave out the news. There was an element of elation in the realization that we had perfected this devastating weapon for employment against an enemy who started the war and has told us she would rather be destroyed than surrender, but it was grim elation. There was sobering awareness of the tremendous responsibility involved.

Secretary Stimson said that this new weapon "should prove a tremendous aid in the shortening of the war against Japan," and there were other responsible officials who privately thought that this was an extreme understatement, and that Japan might find herself unable to stay in the war under the coming rain of atom bombs.

It was obvious that officials at the highest levels made the important decision to release news of the atomic bomb because of the psychological effect it may have in forcing Japan to surrender. However, there are some officials who feel privately it might have been well to keep this completely secret. Their opinion can be summed up in the comment by one spokesman: "Why bother with psychological warfare against an enemy that already is beaten and hasn't sense enough to quit and save herself from utter doom?"

The first news came from President Truman's office. Newsmen were summoned and the historic statement from the Chief Executive, who still is on the high seas, was given to them.

"That bomb," Mr. Truman, said, "had more power than 20,000 tons of TNT. It had more than 2,000 times the blast power of the British 'Grand Slam,' which is the largest bomb (22,000 pounds) ever yet used in the history of warfare."

EXPLOSIVE CHARGE IS SMALL

No details were given on the plane that carried the bomb. Nor was it stated whether the bomb was large or small. The President, however, said the explosive charge was "exceedingly small." It is known that tremendous force is packed into tiny quantities of the element that constitutes these bombs. Scientists, looking to the peacetime uses of atomic power, envisage submarines, ocean liners and planes traveling around the world on a few pounds of the element. Yet, for various reasons, the bomb used against Japan could have been extremely large.

Hiroshima, first city on earth to be the target of the "Cosmic Bomb," is a city of 318,000, which is — or was — a major quartermaster depot and port of embarkation for the Japanese. In addition to large military supply depots, it manufactured ordnance, mainly large guns and tanks, and machine tools and aircraft-ordnance parts.

President Truman grimly told the Japanese that "the end is not yet."

"In their present form these bombs are now in production," he said, "and even more powerful forms are in development."

He sketched the story of how the late President Roosevelt and Prime Minister Churchill agreed that it was wise to concentrate research in America, and how great, secret cities sprang up in this country, where, at one time, 125,000 men and women labored to harness the atom. Even today more than 65,000 workers are employed.

"What has been done," he said, "is the greatest achievement of organized science in history.

"We are now prepared to obliterate more rapidly and completely every productive enterprise the Japanese have above ground in any city. We shall destroy their docks, their factories and their communications. Let there be no mistake; we shall completely destroy Japan's power to make war."

The President emphasized that the atomic discoveries were so important, both for the war and for the peace, that he would recommend to Congress that it consider promptly establishing "an appropriate commission to control the production and use of atomic power within the United States."

"I shall give further consideration and make further recommendations to the Congress as to how atomic power can become a powerful and forceful influence toward the maintenance of world peace," he said.

Secretary Stimson called the atomic bomb "the culmination of years of herculean effort on the part of science and industry, working in cooperation with the military authorities." He promised that "improvements will be forthcoming shortly which will increase by several fold the present effectiveness."

"But more important for the long-range implications of this new weapon," he said, "is the possibility that another scale of magnitude will be developed after considerable research and development. The scientists are confident that over a period of many years atomic bombs may well be developed which will be very much more powerful than the atomic bombs now at hand."

INVESTIGATION STARTED IN 1939

It was late in 1939 that President Roosevelt appointed a commission to investigate use of atomic energy for military purposes. Until then only small-scale research with Navy funds had taken place. The program went into high gear.

By the end of 1941 the project was put under direction of a group of eminent American scientists in the Office of Scientific Research and Development, under Dr. Vannevar Bush, who reported directly to Mr.

Roosevelt. The President also appointed a General Policy Group, consisting of former Vice President Henry A. Wallace, Secretary Stimson, Gen. George C. Marshall, Dr. James B. Conant, president of Harvard, and Dr. Bush. In June, 1942, this group recommended vast expansion of the work and transfer of the major part of the program to the War Department.

Maj. Gen. Leslie R. Groves, a native of Albany, N.Y., and a 48-year-old graduate of the 1918 class at West Point, was appointed by Mr. Stimson to take complete executive charge of the program. General Groves, an engineer, holding the permanent Army rank of lieutenant colonel, received the highest praise from the War Department for the way he "fitted together the multifarious pieces of the vast country-wide jigsaw," and, at the same time, organized the virtually air-tight security system that kept the project a secret.

A military policy committee also was appointed, consisting of Dr. Bush, chairman; Dr. Conant, Lieut. Gen. Wilhelm D. Styer and Rear Admiral William R. Purnell.

In December, 1942, the decision was made to proceed with construction of large-scale plants. Two are situated at the Clinton Engineer Works in Tennessee and a third at the Hanford Engineer Works in the State of Washington.

These plants were amazing phenonema in themselves. They grew into large, self-sustaining cities, employing thousands upon thousands of workers. Yet, so close was the secrecy that not only were the citizens of the area kept in darkness about the nature of the project, but the workers themselves had only the sketchiest ideas — if any — as to what they were doing. This was accomplished, Mr. Stimson said, by "compartmentalizing" the work so "that no one has been given more information than was absolutely necessary to his particular job."

The Tennessee reservation consists of 59,000 acres, eighteen miles west of Knoxville; it is known as Oak Ridge and has become a modern small city of 78,000, fifth largest in Tennessee.

In the State of Washington the Government has 430,000 acres in an isolated area, fifteen miles northwest of Pasco. The settlement there, which now has a population of 17,000, consisting of plant operators and their immediate families, is known as Richland.

A special laboratory also has been set up near Santa Fe, N.M, under direction of Dr. J. Robert Oppenheimer of the University of California. Dr. Oppenheimer also supervised the first test of the atomic bomb on July 16, 1945. This took place in a remote section of the New Mexico desert lands, with a group of eminent scientists gathered, frankly fearful to witness the results of the invention, which might turn out to be either the salvation or the Frankenstein's monster of the world.

Mr. Stimson also gave full credit to the many industrial corporations and educational institutions which worked with the War Department in bringing this titanic undertaking to fruition.

In August, 1943, a combined policy committee was appointed, consisting of Secretary Stimson, Drs. Bush and Conant for the United States; the late Field Marshal Sir John Dill (now replaced by Field Marshal Sir Henry Maitland Wilson) and Col. J. J. Llewellin (since replaced by Sir Ronald Campbell), for the United Kingdom, and C. D. Howe for Canada.

"Atomic fission holds great promise for sweeping developments by which our civilization may be enriched when peace comes, but the overriding necessities of war have precluded the full exploration of peacetime applications of this new knowledge," Mr. Stimson said. "However, it appears inevitable that many useful contributions to the well-being of mankind will ultimately flow from these discoveries when the world situation makes it possible for science and industry to concentrate on these aspects."

Although warning that many economic factors will have to be considered "before we can say to what extent atomic energy will supplement coal, oil and water as fundamental sources of power," Mr. Stimson acknowledged that "we are at the threshold of a new industrial art which will take many years and much expenditure of money to develop."

The Secretary of War disclosed that he had appointed an interim committee to study post-war control and development of atomic energy. Mr. Stimson is serving as chairman, and other members include James F. Byrnes, Secretary of State; Ralph A. Bard, former Under-Secretary of the Navy; William L. Clayton, Assistant Secretary of State; Dr. Bush, Dr. Conant, Dr. Carl T. Compton, chief of the Office of Field Service in OSRD and president of Massachusetts Institute of Technology, and George L. Harrison, special consultant to the Secretary of War and president of the New York Life Insurance Company. Mr. Harrison is alternate chairman of the committee.

The committee also has the assistance of an advisory group of some of the country's leading physicists, including Dr. Oppenheimer, Dr. E. O. Lawrence, Dr. A. H. Compton and Dr. Enrico Fermi. The War Department gave this supplementary background on the development of the atomic bomb:

"The series of discoveries which led to development of the atomic bomb started at the turn of the century when radioactivity became known to science. Prior to 1939 the scientific work in this field was world-wide, but more particularly so in the United States, the United Kingdom, Germany, France, Italy and Denmark. One of Denmark's great scientists, Dr. Neils Bohr, a Nobel Prize winner, was whisked from the grasp of the Nazis in his occupied homeland and later assisted in developing the atomic bomb.

"It is known that Germany worked desperately to solve the problem of controlling atomic energy."

Which Date Should Live in Infamy?

OPINION | BY JON MEACHAM | DEC. 10, 2016

WINSTON CHURCHILL was ebullient; he thought it was all over at last. On the evening of Sunday, Dec. 7, 1941, hosting a small birthday dinner at Chequers, the prime minister's country retreat, for Kathleen Harriman, the daughter of the American diplomat W. Averell Harriman, Churchill heard the news of the Japanese attack on Pearl Harbor from the BBC. "At this very moment I knew the United States was in the war, up to the neck and in to the death," he wrote in his war memoirs. "So we had won after all!" After standing alone against Berlin since the German invasion of Poland on the first day of September 1939, struggling to engage an isolationist America, Churchill "slept the sleep of the saved and thankful."

So the prevailing story of World War II goes even now, 75 years later. The attack on Pearl Harbor, an occasion of ceremonial remembrance commemorated once more last week, propelled the United States into the global contest against Japanese imperialism and European totalitarianism; within four years a once-isolationist America would achieve a superpower status from which it has yet to fall.

Yet the reality, as usual, is more complicated. The story of America's entry into World War II three-quarters of a century ago offers us a window into the contingencies of history and the perennial risk that the nation's isolationist tendencies — tendencies once more evident in our politics as the president-elect of the United States in 2016 revives the old slogan America First — can be durably potent even in moments of existential crisis.

In reaction to the bloodshed of World War I and to the cataclysm of the Great Depression — a global phenomenon — the United States spent the interwar years deeply skeptical of engagement overseas. Constricted by neutrality acts produced by isolationist sentiment and by the popular agitation of groups such as America First, Franklin D.

Roosevelt was forced to maneuver carefully as the Nazi threat grew in Europe. For 27 months, from the invasion of Poland through the Battle of Britain, the fall of France, the U-boat war in the Atlantic and Hitler's invasion of the Soviet Union, America was the most reluctant of warriors.

With the news of Pearl Harbor, Churchill, who had long — and largely unsuccessfully — wooed Roosevelt, believed he now had a full partner in the war against the Axis. "He was quite naturally in a high state of excitement," noted Anthony Eden, the foreign secretary. Churchill was eager to travel to Washington to lay plans for Allied strategy. Eden, however, "was not sure that the Americans would want him so soon."

Eden was right. When Roosevelt dictated his speech declaring war on Japan to his secretary Grace Tully, it concerned only one nation: Japan. Cabinet members, including Secretary of State Cordell Hull and Secretary of War Henry Stimson, wanted F.D.R. to move against Hitler, but the president's political instincts told him to hold off. In a conversation with the British ambassador in Washington, Lord Halifax, Roosevelt was explicit about his concerns: "I seem to be conscious of a still lingering distinction in some quarters of the public between war with Japan and war with Germany."

Isolationist opinion about the Pacific had evaporated in the heat of Pearl Harbor; it was less certain whether Americans were willing to engage fully in Europe as well. From its national headquarters in Chicago, America First was disbanding and released a statement supporting war against Japan, but, as the historian Wayne S. Cole has written, the isolationist group's remarks were deliberately "phrased to leave the door open for possible continued opposition to participation in the European war."

From afar, frustrated by the Eastern Front, Hitler solved Roosevelt's problem by unilaterally declaring war on the United States on Thursday, Dec. 11.

Hitler's motives remain mysterious. He was bound to join Japan under the Tripartite Pact only if Japan had been attacked, and treaties never meant that much to the Führer in any event. The best historical thinking is that Hitler believed he could win the war against American shipping in the Atlantic if he had a free hand, and he apparently decided that Japan's bold stroke in the Pacific gave him the opening he needed to control the Atlantic.

And there was his grandiose vision of the destiny of National Socialism. "I understand only too well that a worldwide distance separates Roosevelt's ideas and my ideas," Hitler said in his speech declaring war. "Roosevelt comes from a rich family and belongs to the class whose path is smoothed in the democracies. I was the only child of a small, poor family and had to fight my way by work and industry." As for Germany, "It needs charity neither from Mr. Roosevelt nor from Mr. Churchill," he said. "It wants only its rights! It will secure for itself this right to live even if thousands of Churchills and Roosevelts conspire against it."

Hitler had badly misjudged Roosevelt's nation. "I don't see much future for the Americans," Hitler said in January 1942. "Everything about the behavior of American society reveals that it's half Judaized, and the other half Negrified. How can one expect a state like that to hold together?"

What Hitler saw as America's fatal weakness — our diversity — was of course the nation's ultimate strength. That he had to force America's hand by making his declaration of Dec. 11 before the United States could itself decide to make war on Nazi Germany is an uncomfortable reminder of the truth of an old observation attributed to the thankful Winston Churchill: One can always count on the Americans to do the right thing — after we've exhausted every other possibility.

JON MEACHAM IS THE AUTHOR, AMONG OTHER BOOKS, OF "FRANKLIN AND WINSTON: AN INTIMATE PORTRAIT OF AN EPIC FRIENDSHIP."

At the Site of Germany's Biggest World War II Battle, a Changing View of History

BY ALISON SMALE | JULY 18, 2017

SEELOW, GERMANY — In the best mellow spirit of modern Germany, the local authorities in Seelow wanted to build a bike path so the increasing number of tourists could expand their rides across the tranquil flat plain of the Oder River and into neighboring Poland.

This being the site of the biggest World War II battle on German soil, a team was chosen to scour the proposed bike path route for abandoned ordnance. Soon they turned up not munitions, but a mass grave, with the remains of as many as 28 Soviet soldiers.

The finding, in May, confirmed once more the blood-soaked nature of the Oder plain, where tens of thousands of soldiers on the Soviet and Nazi sides perished in the April 1945 battle for the Seelow Heights. The rocky outcrop rises just 100 meters above the plain, about 325 feet, but it gave some 80,000 Germans sufficient cover to dig in and slaughter many of the up to one million Soviet troops sent in waves to overwhelm the enemy and clear the way to Berlin.

This history has never ceased to leave its mark, making Seelow a showcase for that unfailing truth of war: To the victors go the spoils, especially the chance to impose their version of events.

After the Allies crushed Hitler, Seelow Heights became a showcase for Stalin. Two Soviet sculptors, Lev Kerbel and Vladimir Zigal, created a bronze statue of a Red Army soldier, gazing mournfully toward his homeland, said the monument's director, Kerstin Niebsch.

The figure conveys a "more in sorrow than anger" mood while leaving no doubt of superiority — moral and military — as it towers over the land of vanquished Nazi Germany. Below the statue and the cliff where it is mounted stand the neat graves of 66 fallen Soviet soldiers, as young as 19, with headstones bearing black stars, not the usual Communist red.

It is a powerful sight, bordered by trees and a stunning view of the plain where these men met their deaths. As Ms. Niebsch noted to several visitors on a recent Sunday, it is a spot that shows just how worthless human life can become. "Even really hardened men," like a recent group of officers from Georgia, the former Soviet republic, "swallow hard."

Next in the layers of history to peel back is the East German period, 1972 to 1989. As the Soviets in general somewhat relaxed their grip on the Communist state in Germany, control of Seelow's memorial site passed then to the local authorities.

A museum was built of wood logs and small windows with iron grids, an echo of the trenches the Nazis dug before the Soviet charge. The East German Army held elaborate swearing-in ceremonies here, complete with torchlight parades.

The emphasis was on unbreakable Soviet-East German friendship. Red marble gravestones with the names of fallen Soviet soldiers were moved in next to the 1945 cemetery.

In a sign of the bungling that eventually led East Germany's Communists to their fall, the remains of the Soviet veterans named on those headstones were not transferred here in the 1970s, but only in 2006 after the mistake came to light.

The East Germans also proudly displayed one of the powerful lights Marshal Georgi P. Zhukov used to illuminate the battlefield when he ordered his troops to advance in the predawn hours of April 16, 1945.

It was only after the fall of the Berlin Wall that it was openly admitted that those lights, instead of aiding the Soviet charge, in fact blinded the Red Army and highlighted Soviet silhouettes for the Nazis to shoot at because of light reflecting off clouds of battlefield smoke.

Despite his long-concealed blunders, Marshal Zhukov did eventually prevail, and took Berlin, albeit a week after Stalin's target of May 1, the International Day of Labor.

A statue of a Red Army soldier at the memorial in Germany for the Seelow Heights attack in 1945. A mass grave was discovered in May, and several hundred bodies are discovered or reburied each year in this region.

Today, Seelow Heights reflects the post-Communist unease of a Cold War that has passed but left unfinished business.

In Russia, where political changes have long rendered the past unpredictable, the Orthodox Church, which survived atheist Communism, has emerged as a staunch supporter of honoring fallen Soviet soldiers, as a display near a magnificent dark marble Orthodox cross explains.

Like other embassies of the old Allied forces in Berlin, Russia's maintains an attaché for war graves and the hundreds of Soviet graveyards in Germany.

Despite the many problems in the West's dealings with the Kremlin these days, cooperation between Germans and Russians — volunteers and officials — is intact, contributing to yet another view of the significance of Seelow, as a symbol of reconciliation.

Yevgeny A. Aleshin, the Russian attaché for war graves, said he hoped the bodies found in May would be buried with due ceremony next year in a nearby cemetery. Several hundred bodies are discovered or reburied each year in this region, he noted.

Since reunification, Germany has carved out a reputation for confronting its history. The telling of the war's chaos and horror has accorded a big role to witnesses like Günter Debski, 89, who visit schools and recount tales backed up, in his case, by carefully preserved scraps of paper, photos and a piece of shrapnel retrieved from the remnants of a backpack that saved his life.

Mr. Debski survived several brushes with death in 1945. He was forced to fight for the Nazis, was captured by the Red Army, marched to the Russian border at Brest and was then freed to make his own way back to Berlin. Eventually, he was police chief for 10 years in the East German city of Eisenhüttenstadt.

As he sat one recent morning in a local hotel, his stories sent a chill through the sunlit room.

"All of a sudden, it just erupted," he said of the Soviet charge on Seelow Heights on April 16, 1945. "There was shooting. Everything shuddered, I just could not imagine what was happening. I thought, perhaps an earthquake. Nothing resembled it — perhaps only the bombing in Dresden," he said, referring to the Allied air assault there in February 1945, which he also witnessed.

Unforgettable, Mr. Debski said, was the loud "hurrah" with which the Soviets charged despite the German artillery fire.

What will happen to history when the last survivors die is a big and unanswered question. Bored teenagers and other children seen in three recent visits to Seelow Heights suggested a need for a more lively 21st century presentation than the static and detailed written displays that are a staple of Germany's painstaking chronicling of the Nazi or Communist past.

Older visitors, while too young to have known the war or the Holocaust, know why they have come to Seelow.

"Many people died here," said Benjamin Langhammer, 54, a musician from Erfurt who had visited once 10 years ago with his father and was now stopping off during a solo bike tour.

"We had a lot of history told us" during Communist East German times, he noted. "And you always know you are only getting half the story, the one the winners tell."

It was important to correct distortions, he said. Although "as a German, the last thing you should do is try to lecture someone else. Right?"

VICTOR HOMOLA CONTRIBUTED REPORTING.

CHAPTER 3

The Vietnam War

The Vietnam War was technically a civil war between communist North Vietnam and South Vietnam. However, the involvement of the United States and the Soviet Union resulted in a protracted conflict that ultimately claimed more than 50,000 American lives. The war was hugely unpopular domestically, sparking massive protests against the draft and the validity of the conflict. In 1971, The New York Times published The Pentagon Papers, detailing a series of deceptions about the United States' engagement in the conflict.

160 U.S. and Saigon Planes Bomb 2 Bases in North in Record Raid

BY JACK LANGGUTH | MARCH 3, 1965

SAIGON, SOUTH VIETNAM, MARCH 2 — More than 100 United States jet aircraft bombed a North Vietnamese munitions depot today and also provided air cover for 60 South Vietnamese bombers striking at a Communist naval base.

The naval base, at Quanghke, although farther north in North Vietnam than any target hit within the last month, was part of a military complex in the southern third of the country.

The raids on Quanghke and the munitions depot at Xombang were the first that did not follow immediately upon an attack by Vietcong guerrillas in South Vietnam against American installations.

[President Johnson said that six planes had been shot down during the missions but that five of the pilots had been rescued, United Press

International reported. It also said North Vietnam's Hanoi radio had asserted that, in addition to the six aircraft downed, "many others" were damaged.]

PILOTS ARE PICKED UP

The missions were carried out by the largest number of planes yet used in one day against targets in North Vietnam. In the single strike of Feb. 11 the number involved was also given as more than 160, but United States Air Force officials said today's total was greater.

The pilots of the downed planes, one of whom was a Vietnamese, were picked up by United States Navy aircraft.

The attacks followed by a day a declaration by Premier Phan Huy Quat that there could be no peace until "the Communists end the war they have provoked and stop their infiltration." The Premier spoke out as talk of peace through negotiations was increasing in Saigon.

The strikes also followed an unrelated disclosure earlier in the day that three United States jets accidentally bombed South Vietnamese Government forces last Sunday, killing four soldiers and wounding 15.

The step-up in the war indicated by the raids was further underlined by reports that a United States Marine unit would be landed on the coast of South Vietnam later this week to provide security for the air base at Danang.

According to Col. Hal L. Price of Orlando, Fla., the director of operations for the Second Air Division in Saigon, the targets were hit at about 3:45 PAL and the last planes had returned to Danang by 6 o'clock.

The Quangkhe naval base, bombed by the South Vietnamese planes, is about 65 miles north of the 17th Parallel, which forms the border between North and South Vietnam. The Xombang munitions depot is about 10 miles inside North Vietnam.

Colonel Price said the missions had been "without doubt very successful." The targets were "really well beat up," he, added, estimating that 70 to 80 per cent of both had been destroyed.

About 70 tons of bombs were dropped on Quangkhe, the colonel said, and more than 120 tons at Xombang. He described the bombs as "conventional general-purpose ordnance," weighing from 250 to 750 pounds.

Pilots reported ground fire that they termed "light and not accurate" despite the aircraft that were lost.

Colonel Price suggested that the absence of heavy air defenses indicated "that the element of surprise is still there."

In addition to the supply and administrative buildings bombed at Quangkhe, the South Vietnamese A-1H Skyraiders sank three to five small vessels at the port Colonel Price said.

They were accompanied by United States jet fighters for suppression of antiaircraft fire. F-100's, F-105's and B-57's made the raid at Xombang without Vietnamese participation.

A spokesman for the American mission denied that the strikes, the fourth and fifth in the last month, represented a change in United States Policy.

He said that the bombing raids of Feb. 7, 8 and 11 had not been specifically provoked by Communist bombing and mortar attacks on American barracks at Pleiku and Quinhon.

Seeking to avoid the impression that the United States only responded to assaults on Americans, Ambassador Maxwell D. Taylor has said several times recently that the bombing raids were replies to "the continuous aggressive acts" by Hanoi.

JOINT STATEMENT ON RAID

A joint statement issued today by South Vietnam and the United States mission cited the discovery of a North Vietnamese arms ships last Feb. 16 in Vungro Bay as "conclusive new evidence of Hanoi's aggression."

The statement also mentioned "two examples of recent terrorism" by the Vietcong that it said had been taken from a long list of Communist actions. The most recent, it said, occurred Feb. 22.

A United States spokesman declined to say when the mimeographed text had been prepared but it had clearly been ready for some time.

Informed American sources said the missions had been sceduled for last Friday but delayed because of bad weather.

Attached to the statement was a second page dated March 2, 1965. It asked "newsmen having knowledge of aircraft taking off on strikes against North Vietnam or of such strikes actually in progress voluntarily to refrain from filing such information or discussing it over,communications facilities until the aircraft have returned."

The request, made in the name of Barry Zorthian, the United States Embassy's minister-counselor for public affairs, indicated that further strikes were planned. But the American mission spokesman declined all comment on further military actions.

McNamara Report to Johnson on the Situation in Saigon in '63

BY THE NEW YORK TIMES | JUNE 13, 1971

Following are the texts of key documents accompanying the Pentagon's study of the Vietnam war for the period December, 1963, through the Tonkin Gulf incident in August, 1964, and its aftermath. Except where excerpting is specified, the documents are printed verbatim, with only unmistakable typographical errors corrected.

MEMORANDUM, "Vietnam Situation," from Secretary of Defense Robert McNamara to President Lyndon B. Johnson, Dec. 21, 1963.

In accordance with your request this morning, this is a summary of my conclusions after my visit to Vietnam on December 19–20.

1. **Summary.** The situation is very disturbing. Current trends, unless reversed in the next 2–3 months, will lead to neutralization at best and more likely to a Communist controlled state.

2. **The new government** is the greatest source of concern. It is indecisive and drifting. Although Minh states that he, rather than the Committee of Generals, is making decisions, it is not clear that this is actually so. In any event, neither he nor the Committee are experienced in political administration and so far they show little talent for it. There is no clear concept on how to reshape or conduct the strategic hamlet program; the Province Chiefs, most of whom are new and inexperienced, are receiving little or no direction because the generals are so preoccupied with essentially political affairs. A specific example of the present situation is that General [name illegible] is spending little or no time commanding HI Corps, which is in the vital zone around Saigon and needs full time direction. I made these points as strongly as possible to Minh, Don, Kim, and Tho.

3. The Country Team is the second major weakness. It lacks leadership, has been poorly informed, and is not working to a common plan. A recent example of confusion has been conflicting USOM and military recommendations both to the Government of Vietnam and to Washington on the size of the military budget. Above all, Lodge has virtually no official contact with Harkins. Lodge sends in reports with major military implications without showing them to Harkins, and does not show Harkins important incoming traffic. My impression is that Lodge simply does not know how to conduct a coordinated administration. This has of course been stressed to him both by Dean Rusk and myself (and also by John McCone), and I do not think he is consciously rejecting our advice; he has just operated as a loner all his life and cannot readily change now.

Lodge's newly designated deputy, David Nes, was with us and seems a highly competent team player. I have stated the situation frankly to him and he has said he would do all he could to constitute what would in effect be an executive committee operating below the level of the Ambassador.

As to the grave reporting weakness, both Defense and CIA must take major steps to improve this. John McCone and I have discussed it and are acting vigorously in our respective spheres.

4. Viet Cong progress has been great during the period since the coup, with my best guess being that the situation has in fact been deteriorating in the countryside since July to a far greater extent than we realized because of our undue dependence on distorted Vietnamese reporting. The Viet Cong now control very high proportions of the people in certain key provinces, particularly those directly south and west of Saigon. The Strategic Hamlet Program was seriously overextended in those provinces, and the Viet Cong has been able to destroy many hamlets, while others have been abandoned or in some cases betrayed or pillaged by the government's own Self Defense Corps. In these key provinces, the Viet Cong have destroyed almost all major roads, and are collecting taxes at will.

As remedial measures, we must get the government to reallocate its military forces so that its effective strength in these provinces is essentially doubled. We also need to have major increases in both military and USOM staffs, to sizes that will give us a reliable, independent U.S. appraisal of the status of operations. Thirdly, realistic pacification plans must be prepared, allocating adequate time to secure the remaining government controlled areas and work out from there.

This gloomy picture prevails predominantly in the provinces around the capital and in the Delta. Action to accomplish each of these objectives was started while we were in Saigon. The situation in the northern and central areas is considerably better, and does not seem to have deteriorated substantially in recent months. General Harkins still hopes these areas may be made reasonably secure by the latter half of next year.

In the gloomy southern picture, an exception to the trend of Viet Cong success may be provided by the possible adherence to the government of the Cao Dai and Hoa Hao sects, which total three million people and control key areas along the Cambodian border. The Hoa Hao have already made some sort of agreement, and the Cao Dai are expected to do so at the end of this month. However, it is not clear that their influence will be more than neutralized by these agreements, or that they will in fact really pitch in on the government's side.

5. Infiltration of men and equipment from North Vietnam continues using (a) land corridors through Laos and Cambodia; (b) the Mekong River water ways from Cambodia; (c) some possible entry from the sea and the tip of the Delta. The best guess is that 1000–1500 Viet Cong cadres entered South Vietnam from Laos in the first nine months of 1963. The Mekong route (and also the possible sea entry) is apparently used for heavier weapons and ammunition and raw materials which have been turning up in increasing numbers in the south and of which we have captured a few shipments.

To counter this infiltration, were viewed in Saigon various plans providing for crossborder operations into Laos. On the scale proposed,

I am quite clear that these would not be politically acceptable or even militarily effective. Our first need would be immediate U2 mapping of the whole Laos and Cambodian border, and this we are preparing on an urgent basis.

One other step we can take is to expand the existing limited but remarkably effective operations on the Laos side, the so-called Operation HARD NOSE, so that it at least provides reasonable intelligence on movements all the way along the Laos corridor; plans to expand this will be prepared and presented for approval in about two weeks.

As to the waterways, the military plans presented in Saigon were unsatisfactory, and a special naval team is being sent at once from Honolulu to determine what more can be done. The whole waterway system is so vast, however, that effective policing may be impossible.

In general, the infiltration problem, while serious and annoying, is a lower priority than the key problems discussed earlier. However, we should do what we can to reduce it.

6. Plans for Covert Action into North Vietnam were prepared as we had requested and were an excellent job. They present a wide variety of sabotage and psychological operations against North Vietnam from which I believe we should aim to select those that provide maximum pressure with minimum risk. In accordance with your direction at the meeting, General Krulak of the JCS is chairing a group that will lay out a program in the next ten days for our consideration.

7. Possible neutralization of Vietnam is strongly opposed by Minh, and our attitude is somewhat suspect because of editorials by the New York Times and mention by Walter Lippmann and others. We reassured them as strongly as possible on this — and in somewhat more general terms on the neutralization of Cambodia. I recommend that you convey to Minh a Presidential message for the New Year that would also be a vehicle to stress the necessity of strong central direction by the government and specifically by Minh himself.

8. U.S. resources and personnel cannot usefully be substantially increased. I have directed a modest artillery supplement, and also the provision of uniforms for the Self Defense Corps, which is the most exposed force and suffers from low morale. Of greater potential significance, I have directed the Military Departments to review urgently the quality of the people we are sending to Vietnam. It seems to have fallen off considerably from the high standards applied in the original selections in 1962, and the JCS fully agree with me that we must have our best men there.

Conclusion. My appraisal may be overly pessimistic. Lodge, Harkins, and Minh would probably agree with me on specific points, but feel that January should see significant improvement. We should watch the situation very carefully, running scared, hoping for the best, but preparing for more forceful moves if the situation does not show early signs of improvement.

End of a Nightmare

BY THE NEW YORK TIMES | JAN. 24, 1973

THE VIETNAM AGREEMENT announced by President Nixon last night after more than four years of false starts and disappointed hopes could mark a momentous turning point for the United States, for Southeast Asia and for the world. If it does not guarantee peace, this historic pact at least provides the framework and opportunity for a new era of compromise and conciliation in Vietnam and elsewhere. In the President's words, "ending the war is only the first step toward building the peace."

For the United States, the agreement signals the end of a nightmare, the lifting of a staggering burden from the nation's resources, energies and conscience. It promises the speedy and safe return of American troops and prisoners and an opportunity for fresh beginnings on neglected problems at home and abroad.

For the Vietnamese and perhaps for their embattled neighbors, the accord may signify the extrication of their domestic differences from the big power struggle that has tragically overwhelmed them for a generation and a chance to seek their own solutions. The world can only hope that a war-weary people, left to their own devices, will find a peaceful way out of the many problems that remain unresolved.

Meanwhile, the tenacious diplomacy of Henry A. Kissinger and Hanoi's Le Duc Tho has set an example of civility under stress that is a model for would be peacemakers everywhere.

This is not an occasion for wild rejoicing. As one Vietnamese neutralist observed when the imminence of peace was first suggested: "After thirty years of sacrifice and suffering, of rivers of blood and mountains of corpses, there is really, nothing to toast." It is, nevertheless, a time for humble thanks, for cautious hope, for the rededication of all mankind to the principles of peaceful settlement of disputes between men and nations.

The Americans Depart

BY THE NEW YORK TIMES | APRIL 30, 1975

THE UNITED STATES left Vietnam with the same confusion and lack of direction that took this country there in the first place. The scenes of agony and tumult in Saigon yesterday as the helicopters lifted American diplomats and panic-stricken Vietnamese away, add up to one more sorrowful episode at the conclusion of an American — and Vietnamese — tragedy.

Untangling the meaning of the rapid events that have flashed past the American and South Vietnamese people these last few days will be an arduous task for the historians. Too many questions are unanswered in the heat of defeat: too many others will be deliberately obscured in the days — and years — to come, for the protection of reputations and ideals that will not easily be given up.

There surely have been instances of genuine heroism; the marines and helicopter pilots who accomplished the ultimate evacuation, for instance, could hardly have been handed a more difficult task, and they seem to have carried out their part with efficiency and bravery. But a strong note of relief which has been felt in the actions of the final 24 hours reflects the narrowness of the American escape and the fact that no massive military force had to be employed to rescue the last remaining United States personnel.

Furthermore, it is a source of some satisfaction that a large number of people in South Vietnam who had put their personal trust in American servicemen and civilians were able to be removed — though not nearly so many as could have been taken out if the evacuation process had begun as early as it should have.

There is still no convincing explanation why the Administration and Ambassador Graham Martin allowed thousands of American personnel to remain on the spot in Saigon long after their functions had become superfluous. Even when evacuation had started, a thousand

American officials remained and became by their presence a force to obstruct the political bargain that might have prevented a final rout.

For their part, the North Vietnamese military commanders and their southern allies have taken upon themselves a heavy responsibility before their own people by pressing for the surrender which the Saigon Government has now offered.

What could have been an orderly transfer of power by procedures internationally agreed upon in the Paris accords of 1973 now appears to have become a simple takeover by force — despite the assurances which Vietnamese Communists had been giving that they were ready for a compromise solution short of open surrender.

Why this change of heart came about is another of the questions which cannot now be answered. But its consequences could be crucial for the future well-being of the Vietnamese people. The Vietnamese Communists will only compound the problems which they obviously face by imposing their idea of a military solution if they shun the readiness of this country to participate in the rebuilding of Vietnam in peace.

What Was the Vietnam War About?

OPINION | BY CHRISTIAN G. APPY | MARCH 26, 2018

WAS AMERICA'S WAR in Vietnam a noble struggle against Communist aggression, a tragic intervention in a civil conflict, or an imperialist counterrevolution to crush a movement of national liberation? Those competing interpretations ignited fiery debates in the 1960s and remain unresolved today. How we name and define this most controversial of American wars is not a narrow scholarly exercise, but profoundly shapes public memory of its meaning and ongoing significance to American national identity and foreign policy.

During the war years, America's leaders insisted that military force was necessary to defend a sovereign nation — South Vietnam — from external Communist aggression. As President Lyndon B. Johnson put it in 1965, "The first reality is that North Vietnam has attacked the independent nation of South Vietnam. Its object is total conquest."

Even more disturbing, Johnson quickly added (following a script written by his predecessors Harry Truman, Dwight Eisenhower and John F. Kennedy), the Communists in Vietnam were supported and guided by the Soviet Union and China. Therefore, the war in South Vietnam was not an isolated, local conflict, irrelevant to American national security, but rather one that was inseparable from the nation's highest priority — the Cold War struggle to contain Communism around the globe. Further raising the stakes, policymakers warned that if South Vietnam fell to Communism, neighboring countries would inevitably fall in turn, one after another, like a row of dominoes.

Three decades later, Robert McNamara, a key architect of the Vietnam War who served as defense secretary for both Presidents Kennedy and Johnson, renounced those wartime claims — the very ones he and others had invoked to justify the war. In two books, "In Retrospect" (1995) and "Argument Without End" (2000), McNamara conceded that the United States had been "terribly wrong" to intervene in Vietnam. He attributed the failure to a lack of knowledge and judgment. If only he had understood the fervor of Vietnamese nationalism, he wrote, if only he had known that Hanoi was not the pawn of Beijing or Moscow, if only he had realized that the domino theory was wrong, he might have persuaded his presidential bosses to withdraw from Vietnam. Millions of lives would have been saved. If only.

In fact, however, in the 1960s, when McNamara advocated massive military escalation in Vietnam, he simply rejected or ignored any evidence that contradicted Cold War orthodoxy. It's not as if contrary views were unavailable. In the work of the scholar-journalist Bernard Fall, the pages of I. F. Stone's Weekly, speeches at university teach-ins and antiwar rallies and countless other venues, critics pointed out that after World War II the United States made a clear choice to support the French effort to re-establish its colonial rule in Indochina, and eventually assumed the bulk of France's cost for the first Indochina War. It should have been no surprise, therefore, that Vietnamese revolutionaries perceived the United States as a neocolonial power when it committed its own military forces in the next war. Moreover, critics argued, the primary roots of opposition to the American-backed government in Saigon were indigenous and deep rooted, not just in North Vietnam, but throughout the South.

Indeed, from the late 1950s through the mid-1960s the bulk of Communist-led fighting was carried out by southern guerrillas of the National Liberation Front, known to its enemies as the Vietcong. Only after the war was well underway did large units from North Vietnam arrive on the southern front. Antiwar opponents also challenged the claim that South Vietnam was an "independent nation" established by the Geneva Accords of 1954. Those agreements called for a temporary partition of Vietnam to be shortly followed by a nationwide election to choose a single leader for a unified Vietnam. When it became clear to both Saigon and Washington that the Communist leader Ho Chi Minh would be the overwhelming victor, the South Vietnamese government of Ngo Dinh Diem, with American support, decided to cancel the election.

Thus began a two-decade failed effort to build a permanent country called "South Vietnam." The government in Saigon was never a malleable puppet of the United States, but it was nonetheless wholly dependent on American military and economic support to survive against its enemies, including many non-Communist parties and factions in the South.

Armed with these criticisms, many opponents of American policy in the 1960s described Vietnam as a civil war — not like the relatively clear-cut North-South division of the American Civil War, but a nationwide struggle of Communist-led forces of the South and North against the American-backed government in the South. By 1966, this analysis was even embraced by some mainstream politicians, including Senator William Fulbright, chairman of the Senate Foreign Relations Committee, and Senator Eugene McCarthy, who ran as an antiwar presidential candidate in 1968. Both men called attention to the "South Vietnamese civil war" to emphasize the strength of the southern insurgency and the failure of the Saigon government to gain the broad support of its own people.

By 1972, the idea that Vietnam posed a threat to Cold War America was so discredited, it sometimes sounded as if America's only remaining war aim was to get back its P.O.W.s (President Richard Nixon bizarrely claimed that Hanoi was using them as "negotiating pawns"). Even more mind-boggling were Nixon's historic 1972 trips to Beijing and Moscow. Many Americans wondered how Nixon could offer toasts of peace to Mao Zedong and Leonid Brezhnev while still waging war in Vietnam. As the journalist Jonathan Schell put it, "If these great powers were not, after all, the true foe," then the war in Vietnam "really was a civil war in a small country, as its opponents had always said, and the United States had no business taking part in it."

But alongside the "civil war" interpretation, a more radical critique developed — the view that America's enemy in Vietnam was engaged in a long-term war for national liberation and independence, first from the French and then the United States. According to this position, the war was best understood not as a Cold War struggle between East and West, or a Vietnamese civil war, but as an anticolonial struggle, similar to dozens of others that erupted throughout the Third World in the wake of World War II. When the French were defeated by Vietnamese revolutionaries (despite enormous American support), the United States stepped in directly to wage a counterrevolutionary war against an enemy determined to achieve full and final independence from foreign control.

This interpretation was shared by many on the antiwar left, including Daniel Ellsberg, the once-hawkish defense analyst who turned so strongly against the war that he was willing to sabotage his career by making public 7,000 pages of classified documents about the history of the Vietnam War, the so-called Pentagon Papers. Ellsberg made his argument most succinctly in the 1974 documentary "Hearts and Minds."

"The name for a conflict in which you are opposing a revolution is counterrevolution," he said. "A war in which one side is entirely financed and equipped and supported by foreigners is not a civil war." The question used to be, he added, "might it be possible that we were on the wrong side in the Vietnamese war. We weren't on the wrong side; we are the wrong side."

In the decades since 1975, all three major interpretations have persisted. Some writers and historians have embraced President Ronald Reagan's view that the war was a "noble cause" that might have been won. That position has failed to persuade most specialists in the field, in large part because it greatly exaggerates the military and political virtues and success of the United States and the government of South Vietnam. It also falls short because it depends on counterfactual claims that victory would have been achieved if only the United States had extended its support for Diem (instead of greenlighting his overthrow), or tried a different military strategy, or done a better job winning hearts and minds. However, the war as it was actually conducted by the United States and its allies was a disaster by every measure.

In recent decades, a number of historians — particularly younger scholars trained in Vietnamese and other languages — have developed various versions of the civil war interpretation. Some of them view the period after the French defeat in 1954 as "post-colonial," a time in which long-brewing internal conflicts between competing versions of Vietnamese nationalism came to a head. As the historian Jessica Chapman of Williams College puts it, "The Vietnam War was, at its core, a civil war greatly exacerbated by foreign intervention." Others have described it as a civil war that became "internationalized."

While these scholars have greatly enhanced our knowledge of the complexity and conflict in Vietnamese history, politics and culture, they don't, in my view, assign enough responsibility to the United States for causing and expanding the war as a neocolonial power.

Let's try a thought experiment. What if our own Civil War bore some resemblance to the Vietnamese "civil war"? For starters, we would have to imagine that in 1860 a global superpower — say Britain — had strongly promoted Southern secession, provided virtually all of the funding for the ensuing war and dedicated its vast military to the battle. We must also imagine that in every Southern state, local, pro-Union forces took up arms against the Confederacy. Despite enormous British support, Union forces prevailed. What would Americans call such a war? Most, I think, would remember it as the Second War of Independence. Perhaps African-Americans would call it the First War of Liberation. Only former Confederates and the British might recall it as a "civil war."

I would reverse Chapman's formula and say that the Vietnam War was, at its core, an American war that exacerbated Vietnamese divisions and internationalized the conflict. It is true, of course, that many Vietnamese opposed the Communist path to national liberation, but no other nationalist party or faction proved capable of gaining enough support to hold power. Without American intervention, it is hard to imagine that South Vietnam would have come into being or, if it did, that it would have endured for long.

Moreover, no other foreign nation deployed millions of troops to South Vietnam (although the United States did pressure or pay a handful of other nations, Australia and South Korea most notably, to send smaller military forces). And no other foreign nation or opponent dropped bombs (eight million tons!) on South and North Vietnam, Cambodia and Laos. The introduction of that staggering lethality was the primary driver of a war that cost three million lives, half of them civilians.

If we continue to excuse American conduct in Vietnam as a well-intentioned, if tragic, intervention rather than a purposeful assertion of imperial power, we are less likely to challenge current war managers who have again mired us in apparently endless wars based on false or deeply misleading pretexts. Just as in the Vietnam era, American leaders have ordered troops to distant lands based on boundless abstractions ("the global war on terror" instead of the global threat of "international Communism"). And once again, their mission is to prop up governments that demonstrate no capacity to gain the necessary support of their people. Once again, the United States has waged brutal counterinsurgencies guaranteed to maim, kill or displace countless civilians. It has exacerbated international violence and provoked violent retaliation.

Our leaders, then and now, have insisted that the United States is "the greatest force for good in the world" that wants nothing for itself, only to defeat "terror" and bring peace, stability and self-determination to other lands. The evidence does not support such a claim. We need a new, cleareyed vision of our global conduct. A more critical appraisal of the past is one place to start.

CHRISTIAN G. APPY IS A PROFESSOR OF HISTORY AT THE UNIVERSITY OF MASSACHUSETTS, AMHERST, AND THE AUTHOR OF "AMERICAN RECKONING: THE VIETNAM WAR AND OUR NATIONAL IDENTITY."

Lyndon Johnson's Vietnam

OPINION | BY MARK K. UPDEGROVE | FEB. 24, 2017

ON THE MORNING of May 27, 1964, a little more than two months before the Gulf of Tonkin Resolution sailed through the House and Senate, allowing the White House the military authority to do what was needed in Southeast Asia, President Lyndon B. Johnson made two phone calls.

The first, which phone logs show he made at 10:55, was with Senator Richard B. Russell, the Georgia Democrat who headed the Armed Services Committee. "What do you think about this Vietnam thing?" Johnson asked the senator, a longtime friend and mentor. "I'd like to hear you talk a little."

"Frankly, Mr. President," Russell replied, "if you were to tell me that I was authorized to settle it as I saw fit, I would respectfully decline to undertake it. It's the damned worst mess I ever saw."

Less than a half-hour later, at 11:24, Johnson called McGeorge Bundy, his national security adviser. "I'll tell you, the more — I just stayed awake last night thinking about this thing — the more I think of it … it looks like to me we're getting into another Korea," he said in a voice of foreboding. "I don't think it's worth fighting for and I don't think wc can get out. And it's just the biggest damn mess."

The president continued, "What the hell is Vietnam worth to me? … What is it worth to this country? … It's damn easy to get in a war, but it's going to be awfully hard to ever extricate yourself if you get in."

These two calls, placed less than a half-hour apart, say everything there is to say about the crisis that would soon shroud Johnson's presidency. The question is, how did a president who understood all of this — and who had people around him to make sure he didn't forget — nevertheless lead the country into a disastrous war?

Johnson had, to be fair, inherited a mess. After the French left Vietnam in 1954 and the country was partitioned, Dwight D. Eisenhower and, after him, John F. Kennedy sent billions in aid and advisers to support the South Vietnamese government under Ngo Dinh Diem. His weak regime needed the money to ward off the Communist insurgency of the Vietcong, a guerrilla force aided by the north's Ho Chi Minh, who had designs to reunify Vietnam. It was an outcome the Americans couldn't accept: According to the so-called domino theory, a Communist victory in Vietnam would inevitably snowball across the region.

And yet Vietnam remained a trouble spot that continued to fester. With the tacit backing of the Kennedy administration, a military coup occurred on Nov. 1, 1963, resulting in Diem's assassination.

It was a move about which Johnson had deep misgivings. "I don't believe assassination is ever justified," he said later. "They were ruthless people. Ho Chi Minh was. But I mean it was ruthless of the United States government, with our boasted list of freedoms, to condone assassination because you don't approve of a political philosophy." Still, after Kennedy's assassination, Johnson dived into Vietnam immediately. "Those first few days," he remembered, "Vietnam was on top of the agenda, before the visiting heads of state got home from the funeral."

His willingness can be explained partly by the man, and partly by his times. Unlike his Democratic Cold War predecessors, Harry S. Truman and Kennedy, Johnson was not so much a student of history as he was of human nature. There he paid attention, picking up on the weaknesses and frailties of those around him in the corridors of power the way a dog senses fear, often exploiting them for political advantage.

Since arriving in Washington in 1934, Johnson had drawn lessons from the world-changing mistakes made by heads of state, especially those that he believed stemmed from weakness. During Johnson's first term as a congressman, in 1938, Prime Minister Neville Chamberlain of Britain appeased Hitler in the belief that he was offering his countrymen "peace for our time," while instead allowing for the German occupation of Czechoslovakia, the unchecked invasion of Poland and the beginning of World War II.

As the war wound down, Franklin D. Roosevelt, in not taking a firmer hand with Stalin at the Yalta Conference — where Allied leaders met to discuss the fate of the postwar world — opened the door for the Soviet domination of Eastern Europe and the Soviets' attempts to spread their influence across the globe.

Truman, Roosevelt's successor, while drawing bold lines in the Cold War through a strict policy of containment, sent troops into battle in Korea without being fully prepared for what lay ahead as American support slipped. For the first time an American war ended in a draw. At the same time, Republicans harshly criticized Truman when the Communist revolutionaries led by Mao took over China as America turned a blind eye. The "Who Lost China?" debate that swept through Washington afterward was less a question than a Republican indictment of Truman and the Democratic Party.

During Eisenhower's eight White House years, while Johnson was Senate minority and then majority leader, the country was defined by its geopolitical position versus the Soviets. Any Soviet gain — a country falling to Communist rule, an American citizen yielding to Communist sympathies — was evidence that the Red Menace was knocking at America's door, giving rise to the domino theory abroad and McCarthyism at home. Fear was the great motivator.

In 1957, when the Soviets showed the world their superiority in space exploration with Sputnik, a satellite no larger than a beach ball, Johnson was a catalyst for improving the country's shoddy space efforts. As he asked rhetorically, "What American wants to go to bed by the light of a Communist moon?"

In 1959, when Cuba's American-backed military dictator, Fulgencio Batista, was overthrown by Fidel Castro's guerrillas, bringing Communism to the Western Hemisphere, Johnson believed the Eisenhower administration hadn't done enough to prevent the insurgency. "Ike sat on his fanny and let them take it by force," he said later.

Kennedy also got into the act as a presidential candidate in 1960, exploiting American fears of a nuclear missile gap with the Soviets, less a reality than a campaign tactic effective enough to win him the White House by the thinnest of margins. Kennedy's inaugural rhetoric — "We shall pay any price, bear any burden, meet any hardship, support any friend, oppose any foe, to assure the survival and success of liberty" — amounted to Cold War bravado. But he would soon stumble with his support of a botched military incursion in Cuba at the Bay of Pigs. Emboldened by Kennedy's humiliation, the Soviets led the United States to the brink of nuclear war a year and a half later as American ships blocked the Soviets from moving nuclear warheads into Cuba.

Weakness, Johnson had seen in three decades in Washington, was never rewarded. When he said of Vietnam, "We're not going to have any men with any umbrellas," a pointed reference to the hapless Chamberlain, the message was clear: America would stand up to Ho Chi Minh and the Vietcong in a way that Chamberlain had not stood up to Hitler and the Nazi regime. For the 36th president, Vietnam began less as a conflict he was determined to win than as one he couldn't afford to lose.

Lyndon Johnson was not going to be the first president to lose a war — and to the Communists, no less. But what began as a reflexive response to support Kennedy's policy in the region, overwhelmingly supported by Congress, his cabinet, and the nation would over time become the central crisis of Johnson's presidency.

Ultimately, despite the consternation he so presciently expressed in the spring of 1964, Vietnam did mean something to Johnson. It became evident with the escalation of American military involvement in the war beginning in 1965. If Johnson had bet much of his presidency on the programs of the Great Society — civil rights, federal aid to education, Medicare, Medicaid, immigration reform — he stacked the balance of his chips fatefully behind the war in Vietnam. And, as he predicted, he found it nearly impossible to "extricate" himself once he got in deep.

MARK K. UPDEGROVE IS THE AUTHOR OF "INDOMITABLE WILL: LBJ IN THE PRESIDENCY."

How Vietnam Changed Journalism

OPINION | BY ANDREW PEARSON | MARCH 29, 2018

WHEN I FIRST got to Saigon as a journalist, in 1963, I took it for granted that American policy to counter Communist expansion into the southern part of Vietnam was the right thing to do. That was the conventional wisdom from experience in Europe, where the Soviet Union had established satellite countries on its border. My journalistic perspective in the beginning was "normal." A good American point of view.

As I learned more about the complexities of the war, my journalism became more accurate. The war's defenders might have said I was becoming more critical, even biased. But in fact I was becoming more objective — I set aside the pro-American, anti-Communist filter I brought with me to Vietnam and reported what I saw. In the news and documentary reports I did, I showed that despite all the destruction, suffering and cost, the war was being lost. Now I'd say it shouldn't have started.

My experience, and that of many, even most, American journalists in the Vietnam War transformed our profession. We realized over the years that the government was ill-informed and even wrong about issues of life and death. As a result of that, reporters today are doing a better job because they know about the evolution of that deception and what its effects have been on American society.

When I realized that nothing was working out the way the United States wanted, I began doing TV programs that showed how bad the situation was. Sometimes people in the New York office said, this can't be right because of what we're hearing from the White House. I was the bad-news messenger. But I could see that the body-count war was being lost. It wasn't possible to kill your way to victory in Vietnam as in World War II. History, culture, the evolution of the Communist Party under Ho Chi Minh — things were different from the situation in Europe.

That breaking point in the "body count" that President Lyndon Johnson wanted, and that Gen. William Westmoreland assured him was close, was a fiction, because those in charge in Hanoi adjusted the level of fighting to suit them, and their young men kept coming because they knew what they were fighting for. President Nguyen van Thieu of South Vietnam never promoted his best officers because he was afraid of a military coup unless he kept his friends in charge of the Army. And the nation-building program, sometimes called pacification, wasn't gaining enough ground to make any difference.

There was no Saigon government in large parts of the country, and it wasn't the fault of people who lived there that South Vietnamese generals had never been able to govern. Elections were sometimes held, but they were rigged public relations efforts for the benefit of Washington. The rural population in the South was like a second country, and those people mostly supported Ho Chi Minh. They had since after World War II, but especially since Ho beat the French Army in 1954. That was their war of independence, but Washington misunderstood the consequences of Ho's victory and decided to reverse it.

Serious journalists today carry with them an awareness of this history — not necessarily the specifics, but the way the media's perception of the war matured — when they start work. They've read David Halberstam's book "The Best and the Brightest," describing the shallow, arrogant views of government officials who didn't think they needed to know that much about Vietnam, and who were too busy to see the country except as a chunk of geography on the map they wanted to control. Reporters today also know how presidents and their advisers, wary about the next election at home, were afraid of losing some piece of the world to "the Communists" and how paranoia served to perpetuate the fighting when the war had already been lost.

They've absorbed the message of Daniel Ellsberg and the Pentagon Papers, revealed through the courageous reporting of Neil Sheehan of The New York Times. They've read the classic books by the historian Bernard Fall on the French and American wars in Indochina. They start off determined to bring insights from the recent past to their reporting about international situations and understand that American elected officials are generally ignorant about other countries.

The Vietnam War has ended up putting an unusual burden on young reporters, their newspapers and TV outlets. Too much stress is placed on reporting the latest incremental turn in a story, especially regarding America's current and brewing conflicts abroad. The news media's business model depends on it. But to serve the public well, the industry needs the time and space to permit reporters to include a larger context in their reporting from abroad. Otherwise, news becomes "Here they come, there they go" linear reporting about military action that doesn't have the meaning it needs to permit Americans to understand where these new conflicts are taking us.

For me, in my old age, the war comes back, out of order, my subconscious offering up memories without my asking. Here's one: that time climbing through a hillside bamboo thicket during a military operation when the heat felt so intense it got inside me, and yet I couldn't seem to drink enough water and was vomiting. I thought I was going to die. Here's another: The troop-carrying choppers settle onto the rice paddy, mud a foot deep, the men move out, tense because this is a Vietcong area, and they burn the village down, even though the enemy isn't shooting at them, ignoring the screaming women and children who are trying to keep the fire from taking everything as they run to haul water from their wells in buckets, throwing it up on their burning thatch.

In 1995, 20 years after the end of the war, I was asked to do an anniversary report. I chose to go to Beallsville, Ohio, a small town that had too many casualties. One of the veterans I went to see, a Marine, came to the door but didn't invite me in or shake my hand. I explained what I was doing, a film for PBS about his experience and the town's loss. He listened, but his expression was hostile. I said I had been in Vietnam myself as a TV reporter for five years over a decade. I tried to think how I could get beyond this awkward moment because sometimes by sharing experience, you can help people realize that you're with them, not against them. But I couldn't overcome his hostility so many years after the war was supposed to be over. I thanked him and left.

I was probably a reminder of all the bad news that had come out of Vietnam, especially on TV. The news was always too brief and too blunt — the ambush, the mine, the wounded, the medevac helicopter trying to come in to get the men out. Then cut to a commercial. His family might have written to him about what they were seeing and asked, is it like that? It was clear that he resented me, maybe hated what he thought was journalistic misrepresentation of the war as he knew it. Or maybe he knew the bad news was correct but didn't want to deal with that either.

There was often resentment among ground troops about "hit and run" reporting — getting news and pictures of the latest firefight by riding helicopters in and out of the battlefield the same day. That style of reporting was a response to pressure from editors back home to get the story out as quickly as possible, to beat the competition, the other wire services, the other networks. Better reporters stuck around for a while, spent the night, shared the combat food rations, the heat and rain, made friends before leaving. So the grunts felt you weren't just using them, like a stage set to entertain the viewers back home with a little bang-bang, as we used to call it.

When the Vietnam War was over, the Pentagon decided that there had been too much negative reporting from the war zone and that it would limit journalists' access to battlefields. Handouts about what had happened would be prepared by public affairs staff, and officers, called "minders," would go along with correspondents to supervise their movements and the information they got. A colleague told me that in Iraq, he wasn't permitted to speak with local people. It's still possible to find out what's actually going on under these restrictive conditions, but it's harder and takes more time. It's also a lot more dangerous now, because wars have become more violent.

Good journalism is always hard to do, but there's a new generation of reporters who take nothing for granted because of what they know about Vietnam. Their work is everywhere in the best daily newspapers, on cable news and in online newsletters, blogs and websites. Of course journalism is populated by an assortment of people. There's no entrance exam, so a lot of reporting is done by people who are ignorant and inexperienced about the subjects they pretend to know. Journalism is no better or worse than any other American institution. But the best young reporters have learned from the Vietnam War to question authority and find out for themselves what's really going on. And that's how it's supposed to work in a democracy.

ANDREW PEARSON IS A JOURNALIST AND TV PRODUCER. HE IS WRITING A MEMOIR.

CHAPTER 4

The Iraq War

In March 2003, as part of the war on terror, the United
States announced its decision to invade Iraq. This decision
was based on information suggesting that Iraq's president. Saddam Hussein, had developed weapons of mass
destruction (WMDs). What followed was a brief military
campaign and years of complex political engagement.
When a fragile Iraqi government was beset with infighting
and the rise of the Islamic State, and reporting revealed
that the WMDs had never existed, the United States was
forced to reckon with the consequences.

Bush Orders Start of War on Iraq; Missiles Apparently Miss Hussein

BY DAVID E. SANGER WITH JOHN F. BURNS | MARCH 20, 2003

PRESIDENT BUSH ordered the start of a war against Iraq on Wednesday
night, and American forces poised on the country's southern border
and at sea began strikes to disarm the country, including an apparently unsuccessful attempt to kill Saddam Hussein.

Mr. Bush addressed the nation from the Oval Office at 10:15 p.m.
Wednesday night, about 45 minutes after the first attacks were
reported against an installation in Baghdad where American intelligence believed Mr. Hussein and his top leadership were meeting. "On
my orders, coalition forces have begun striking selected targets of
military importance to undermine Saddam Hussein's ability to wage
war," the president said.

Speaking deliberately, with a picture of his twin daughters visible behind him, he added, "These are opening stages of what will be a broad and concerted campaign."

Mr. Bush sought to tamp down expectations of a quick victory with few casualties by warning that the battles in the days ahead "could be longer and more difficult than some predict." The results of the strike on Baghdad were unclear. However, Iraqi television broadcast a speech by Mr. Hussein, who is believed to have a number of doubles, after the attack. He denounced "Junior Bush" and promised the Iraqi people a victory.

The president's speech came about two hours after the expiration of his 48-hour deadline for Saddam Hussein to leave Iraq, an ultimatum dismissed with disdain by the Iraqi leader.

The first signs of the attack in Baghdad, which began just before first light there at 5:35 a.m., were an air raid siren followed by anti-aircraft fire and loud explosions over the city that appeared to be bombs. The antiaircraft fire appeared to be ineffective.

At least one impact was visible about a half mile from the Rashid Hotel in central Baghdad, throwing a great cloud of dust into the air.

The initial round of explosions took place over a period of about 10 minutes and was followed by a lull. The first traffic of the day racing down the highway appeared to be drivers fleeing the attack.

It appeared that the war started earlier than the White House and top Pentagon officials had intended. During a nearly four-hour meeting at the White House late Wednesday afternoon — participants included Vice President Cheney; George Tenet, the director of central intelligence; Donald H. Rumsfeld, the secretary of defense; and Condoleezza Rice, the national security adviser — Mr. Bush decided to act on fresh intelligence indicating an opportunity to decapitate the country's leadership early in the war.

It was a chance Mr. Bush missed, to his regret, early in the war in Afghanistan in 2001, when American forces sought to kill Osama bin Laden and the leader of the Taliban, Mullah Omar.

According to two senior military officials, American forces launched about three dozen Tomahawk cruise missiles from four cruisers and destroyers and two submarines operating in the Red Sea and the Persian Gulf as part of an effort to kill Mr. Hussein, his two sons and other senior members of the leadership. Two F-117A Stealth fighters each dropped two one-ton satellite-guided bombs. But the initial attack was described as limited in scope, and fell short of the far more intense strikes to come.

Military officials said the more limited attack was intended to demonstrate that the United States would act on timely intelligence to strike what one official called "targets of opportunity."

"This is not the start of the air campaign," one senior military official said in Washington.

With his four-minute address to the nation, delivered after he finished a quiet dinner with his wife, Laura, in the White House residence, Mr. Bush embarked on one of the country's most ambitious military ventures since Vietnam, and on a war his administration began planning over a year ago.

Many of the hawks in his administration had talked for years of a war like the one that opened tonight, hoping to rid the world of Mr. Hussein, who survived the first gulf war, attempted to assassinate Mr. Bush's father, and killed untold thousands of his opponents.

The president had to act without the sanction of the United Nations Security Council, where he could not assemble the nine votes necessary for a specific authorization to go to war. Germany, France and Russia have declared that the war is, in essence, illegal.

In his speech, Mr. Bush said 35 nations support the United States. But he acted with significant military support from only a small handful of nations led by Britain. A small force was sent by Australia.

"Now that the conflict has come, the only way to limit its duration is to apply decisive force," Mr. Bush said. "And I assure you, this will not be a campaign of half measures and we will accept no outcome but victory."

Mr. Bush argued anew that Mr. Hussein posed a grave threat to the United States, and would attack the country or its interests whenever he gained the weapons and the strength. But he addressed much of his brief speech to the American men and women in the Persian Gulf, telling them that Iraqis "will witness the honorable and decent spirit of the American military." He contended that America had no visions of empire in the Middle East.

"We have no ambition in Iraq," he declared, "except to remove a threat and restore control of that country to its own people."

Earlier Wednesday, Mr. Bush formally informed Congress in writing, and then world leaders in a series of phone calls, that he was ready to depose Mr. Hussein by force. In a seven-page message to Congress, he argued that force was now the only way to "adequately protect the national security of the United States" and that toppling the Iraqi government was "a vital part" of a broader war against terrorism. The message was required under a statute passed last fall explicitly authorizing war against Iraq after the president determined that a diplomatic solution was impossible.

As the deadline passed on Wednesday night, Mr. Bush's dinner was interrupted by a call from Andrew H. Card, the White House chief of staff, Ari Fleischer, the White House press secretary, said. The president asked Mr. Card if there was any evidence that Mr. Hussein had left Iraq. There was none, Mr. Card told him — hardly a surprise after Mr. Hussein's two days of defiant claims that he would stay in place, and defeat the invading army.

Even hours before Mr. Bush addressed the nation, there had been doubt the invasion would start this quickly. As punishing sandstorms swirled around the Army troops massed in Kuwait, the engineering battalions that will be in the vanguard of the invasion force — breaching berms and clearing minefields — were already on the move. Special Operations forces were reportedly already deployed inside Iraq, shaping the battlefield for the larger invasion force to come.

American and British warplanes flew bombing missions today against a dozen Iraqi artillery and surface-to-surface missile positions in southern Iraq, wiping out placements that could threaten advancing troops.

Roughly 17 Iraqi border troops surrendered along the border, and were taken into custody by Kuwaiti forces. A few administration officials seized on the defections as an early indicator of the mass defections they hope to see when the fighting begins.

But others in the administration warned against overconfidence, cautioning that toppling Mr. Hussein and the protective apparatus that has kept him in power for more than three decades is a far riskier enterprise than was ousting his forces from Kuwait 12 years ago in the Persian Gulf war.

Mr. Fleischer cautioned that "Americans ought to be prepared for loss of life." He noted that while the White House sought "as precise, short a conflict as possible," the unknowns — from how American, British and Australian troops would be received to the elements of weather, accident and so-called friendly fire — were numerous.

The notification to Congressional leaders, sent to Capitol Hill late on Tuesday night, provided the most detailed legal justification yet for military action.

Mr. Bush stayed largely out of sight until his speech, save for a brief meeting Wednesday morning with Mayor Michael R. Bloomberg and the secretary of homeland security, Tom Ridge, to review New York City's needs to prepare for any new terrorist attacks. The White House later said it would go to Congress for a special appropriation bill to pay for the war and homeland security.

Washington was eerily quiet, and the area around the White House was sealed off by police.

But there were isolated voices of dissent. "Today, I weep for my country," Senator Robert C. Byrd, the West Virginia Democrat and the war's biggest critic in the Senate, said on Wednesday. "No more is the image of America one of strong, yet benevolent, peacekeeper. Around the globe, our friends mistrust us, our word is disputed, our intentions are questioned."

The breach with Europe continued to widen. As Mr. Bush tried to convince Congress that the attack on Iraq would advance the war on terror, France's foreign minister, Dominique de Villepin, said the war would spawn more terrorism. The German foreign minister, Joschka Fischer, said, "Germany emphatically rejects the impending war."

But while Germany allowed American troops to fly over its territory, Turkey was still arguing about opening its airspace. Turkey further said it would not allow United States forces to use its air bases to refuel — a remarkable slap from a NATO ally. Mr. Fleischer made clear that the $30 billion in proposed aid and loans to Turkey — dangled when it seemed as if the country would allow American and British forces to use its territory to invade Iraq from the north — is "no longer on the table."

Mr. Fleischer disputed the view of Europeans and others who argue that the pending invasion is a violation of the United Nations Charter. He cited three Security Council resolutions that he said provided all of the authorization Mr. Bush needed. But he also likened the current preparations to the Cuban missile crisis in 1962, arguing that just as President Kennedy imposed a quarantine around Cuba — "an act of war," Mr. Fleischer said — to force it to remove nuclear missiles, Mr. Bush is acting to protect the United States from a threat that it would never see coming.

Several scholars have disputed that view, noting that in the case of the missile crisis, the Soviet missiles could have easily reached the United States, and the weapons clearly put Americans at peril.

Mr. Bush argued on Monday night that waiting for the Iraq threat to develop was tantamount to "suicide." The president's definition seemed to fit what scholars say is the classic war of prevention.

"We choose to meet that threat now, where it arises, before it can appear suddenly in our skies and cities," the president said then.

The document submitted to Congress laid out yet another argument — Iraq's links to terrorists, an area in which the administration's evidence has been scanty, and its potential for greater links in the future.

"Both because Iraq harbors terrorists and because Iraq could share weapons of mass destruction with terrorists who seek them for use against the United States, the use of force to bring Iraq into compliance with its obligations under U.N.S.C. resolutions would be a significant contribution to the war on terrorists of global reach," the report to Congress said.

"A change in the current Iraqi regime would eliminate an important source of support for international terrorist activities," it said. "It would likely also assist efforts to disrupt terrorist networks and capture terrorists around the globe. United States government personnel operating in Iraq may discover information through Iraqi government documents and interviews with detained Iraqi officials that would identify individuals currently in the United States and abroad who are linked to terrorist organizations."

That rationale would seem, on its face, to support military action against many nations, from Pakistan to Indonesia. But Mr. Fleischer insisted that the conditions surrounding Iraq's defiance were "unique."

The War Begins

OPINION | BY THE NEW YORK TIMES | MARCH 20, 2003

FROM HERE, the sound of the war that began last night is inaudible. As veterans realize and almost every writer on the subject of war has reminded us, the experience of this new, unwanted war will be unknowable except among those who will be there for the fighting. The job of the soldiers, men and women alike, is transcendently clear. No one who knows the American military doubts that it will do its job to the best of its ability and with an unswerving consciousness of the balance between opportunity and risk. The lives wagered in this operation belong to young Americans and to Iraqis of all ages. Perhaps no military has ever known as well as this one how important it is to have to care for those lives.

Many Americans remember the first gulf war all too vividly, and the temptation will be to read this war against the backdrop of that one. The terrain is the same, but everything else has changed. A military that, even a dozen years ago, still found itself shuttling paper battle orders back and forth is now electronically linked and coordinated in ways that would have seemed unimaginable then. There is no strategic exit in the offing, as there was when the coalition forces stopped well short of Baghdad in 1991. Now it is Saddam or nothing. There is no sense of international coalescence, a mission that bound disparate nations together. This mission has unbound the world.

Our job here is not as transcendently clear as the soldiers' job. Now that the first strikes have begun, even those who vehemently opposed this war will find themselves in the strange position of hoping for just what the president they have opposed is himself hoping for: a quick, conclusive resolution fought as bloodlessly as possible. People who have supported Mr. Bush all along may feel tempted to try to silence those who voice dissent. It will be necessary to remind them that we are in this fight to bring freedom of speech to Iraq, not to smother it back home.

It would take a very set mind to judge what comes next on any ground but the success of the effort. If things go as well as we hope, even those who sharply disagree with the logic behind this war are likely to end up feeling reassured, almost against their will, by the successful projection of American power. Whether they felt the idea of war in Iraq was a bad one from the beginning, or — like us — they felt it should be undertaken only with broad international support, the yearning to go back to a time when we felt in control of our own destiny still runs strong. Of all the reasons for this mission, the unspoken one, deepest and most hopeless, is to erase Sept. 11 from our hearts.

This is now, as Mr. Bush has said repeatedly, a war with two missions: disarming Iraq and then transforming it into a free and hopeful society. That second goal is also an end everyone would like to see. Yet as a nation we have scarcely begun to talk about how it should be accomplished. Even as we sit here at home, worrying about the outcome of the fighting, we must start to debate what comes next.

That public discussion has to start soon, even tomorrow. But for now, all our other thoughts have come to rest. We simply hope for the welfare of those men and women — sons and daughters — who will be flinging themselves into the Iraqi desert.

Wave of Protests, From Europe to New York

BY JOHN TAGLIABUE | MARCH 21, 2003

LEADERS AND PROTESTERS around the world today condemned the start of war in Iraq, with President Jacques Chirac of France warning that it "will be fraught with consequences for the future."

In Russia, President Vladimir V. Putin called for an immediate halt to the American-led assault, saying, "This military action cannot be justified in any way."

Regardless of whether their governments supported or opposed the war, hundreds of thousands massed at protests across Germany, France, Spain, Italy and Britain. In Berlin, an estimated 40,000 demonstrators streamed past the United States Embassy and through the Brandenburg Gate, waving banners that read, "Stop the Bush Fire" and "George W. Hitler."

In the United States, the antiwar demonstrations were generally smaller, but thousands descended on military bases or blocked roads and bridges to voice their opposition. Chanting "Peace Now," some 5,000 people demonstrated in Times Square in New York.

The wave of global protest began even as the first missiles were hitting Baghdad, with tens of thousands in Melbourne, Australia's second city, bringing traffic to a standstill. In the Middle East, demonstrations were scattered — a crowd of only 1,000 in Cairo, for instance — but more vociferous protests were expected on Friday, the day of Muslim worship.

In France, the American Embassy and consulate buildings, just off the Place de la Concorde in Paris, were heavily guarded as tens of thousands of demonstrators assembled, chanting antiwar slogans. The National Assembly briefly suspended its session in symbolic protest.

In Madrid, about 40,000 people packed the Puerta del Sol tonight in protest at the Spanish government's support for President Bush. Fliers that called for a boycott of American consumer goods passed through the crowd.

"At least we can show the world that our government does not represent us," said Javier Velazquez, an economics professor. "It is important to have a European response to a country that just does anything it wants, which is the United States."

American flags were burned outside the embassy in Athens, where an estimated 80,000 demonstrators, mainly students and labor activists, marched peacefully, chanting anti-American slogans.

Sentiment ran generally high against the United States. Fans in Montreal booed loudly tonight when "The Star-Spangled Banner" was sung before the Canadiens' game against the New York Islanders.

Appearing on national television this morning, Mr. Chirac reiterated France's opposition to the war and said he regretted it was "initiated without United Nations backing."

While emphasizing that France was supported by many other nations, he added an appeal for the world and especially Europe to reunite in pursuit of common goals.

"Tomorrow, we shall have to meet again, with our allies, with the whole international community, to take up together the challenges awaiting us," he said. "Europe must realize the need to express its own vision of world problems and support this vision with a credible common defense."

Mr. Chirac spoke before attending a previously scheduled summit meeting of the leaders from the 15 European Union nations in Brussels, where an attempt was made to paper over the continent's deep rifts with a common statement on how best to secure peace after the war in Iraq.

Also attending the summit meeting was Prime Minister Tony Blair of Britain, Mr. Bush's staunchest ally. Before leaving for Brussels, Mr. Blair recorded a five-minute speech that was broadcast in Britain at 10 p.m., formally acknowledging that British troops are now at war.

"I know this course of action has produced deep divisions of opinion in our country," said Mr. Blair, who has faced strong popular protest and a revolt in his Labor Party. "But this new world faces a new threat: of disorder and chaos born either of brutal states like Iraq, armed with weapons of mass destruction, or of extreme terrorist groups. Both hate our way of life, our freedom, our democracy."

Spain's prime minister, José María Aznar, who has also backed Mr. Bush, sent only a hospital ship and 900 personnel to the Persian Gulf. He told his country: "We have assumed our responsibilities. There were more comfortable options, but we don't want to pass on to the future risks that we should confront in the present."

Yet here and there, even among leaders critical of the war, a sense of resignation — and a desire to begin healing divisions — were evident.

In Germany, Chancellor Gerhard Schröder said on television that "the wrong decision was taken." Yet he added, "The differences over the war are clear differences of opinion among governments, not deep-seated differences between friendly peoples."

The New China news agency reported that the former Chinese foreign minister, Tang Jiaxuan, in a telephone call with Secretary of State Colin L. Powell, appealed for an end to military operations, "so that the Iraq issue can be returned to the current track of a political solution."

In Russia, Mr. Putin called the war a "big political mistake."

Mr. Putin, a staunch defender of Russia's sovereignty over the rebel region of Chechnya, said, "If we allow international law to be replaced by the law of the first, in which the strong is always right, and has the right to do anything, then one of the most basic principles of international law will come into question: the inviolability of state sovereignty."

Yet this evening, Russia's foreign minister, Igor S. Ivanov, told reporters that Russia and America "remain partners, not opponents, despite the war in Iraq."

In Canada, Prime Minister Jean Chrétien sought to smooth relations with Washington, saying, "We must do nothing to comfort Saddam Hussein."

"We hope it will be brief, with a minimum of casualties on both sides," Mr. Chrétien said of the war.

In the Pacific, Japan, South Korea and the Philippines, all close allies of the United States, expressed support.

Japan's prime minister, Junichiro Koizumi, despite widespread opposition to the war in Japan, said Baghdad had "not acted sincerely."

The Philippine president, Gloria Macapagal Arroyo, said her country was "part of the coalition of the willing."

But Malaysia and Indonesia, Muslim nations, condemned the war.

Severe condemnation of the war came from the papacy and the leaders of other religions.

In Rome, the papal spokesman, Joaquin Navarro-Valls, said Pope John Paul II was "deeply pained." In a statement, he deplored the fact that Baghdad "did not accept the resolutions of the United Nations and the appeal by the pope himself, which asked for the country to disarm." But he also criticized the rupture of negotiations toward peaceful disarmament.

The papal displeasure was echoed in denunciations of the war from leaders of Catholic, Orthodox, Protestant and Muslim groups.

In South America, official reaction of the six governments making up the Mercosur group, led by Brazil, was uniformly negative. President Luiz Inácio Lula da Silva of Brazil condemned the American position as an act of "disrespect to the United Nations and the rest of the world."

"All of us want for Iraq not to have atomic weapons or weapons of mass destruction," he said, "but that does not give the United States the right to decide by itself what is good and what is bad for the world."

Cheers, Tears and Looting in Capital's Streets

BY JOHN F. BURNS | APRIL 10, 2003

SADDAM HUSSEIN'S rule collapsed in a matter of hours today across much of this capital city as ordinary Iraqis took to the streets in their thousands to topple Mr. Hussein's statues, loot government ministries and interrogation centers and to give a cheering, often tearful welcome to advancing American troops.

After three weeks battling their way north from Kuwait against Mr. Hussein's hard-core loyalists, Army and Marine Corps units moving into the districts of eastern Baghdad where many of the city's five million people live finally met the kind of adulation from ordinary Iraqis that American advocates of a war to topple Mr. Hussein had predicted.

Amid the celebration, many of Mr. Hussein's troops and officials simply abandoned their posts and ran away.

Much of Baghdad became, in a moment, a showcase of unbridled enthusiasm for America, as much as it metamorphosed into a crucible of unbridled hatred for Mr. Hussein and his 24-year rule.

American troops, but almost as much any Westerner caught up in the tide of people rushing into the streets, were met with scenes that summoned comparisons to the freeing of Eastern Europe 14 years ago.

There was no word on the fate of Mr. Hussein or his sons, Uday and Qusay, targeted by American bombs in a western residential area on Monday. But his whereabouts — even his very existence — seemed irrelevant as American Marines used an M88 tank recovery vehicle to topple a large statue of Mr. Hussein in the central Firdos Square.

Crowds surged forward to stomp on the downed statue, whose head had briefly been covered in an American flag, and several men dragged its severed head through the streets.

A burly 39-year-old man named Qifa, assigned by Mr. Hussein's Information Ministry to keep watch on an American reporter, paused at midmorning, outside the inferno that had been the headquarters of Iraq's National Olympic Committee, to ask the reporter to grip his hand. The building, used to torture and kill opponents of Mr. Hussein, had been one of the most widely feared places in Iraq.

"Touch me, touch me, tell me that this is real, tell me that the nightmare is really over," the man said, tears running down his face.

It was real, at last. When the city awoke to find that the American capture on Monday of the government quarter in west Baghdad had been followed overnight by a deep American thrust into the city's eastern half, the fear ingrained in most Iraqis evaporated.

Iraqis on foot, on motor scooters, in cars and minivans and trucks, alone and in groups, children and adults and elderly, headed for any point on the map where American troops had taken up positions — at expressway junctions, outside the United Nations headquarters, at two hotels on the Tigris River where Western journalists had been sequestered by Mr. Hussein's government — and erupted with enthusiasm.

Shouts to the American soldiers of "Thank you, mister, thank you," in English, of "Welcome, my friend, welcome," of "Good, good, good," and "Yes, yes, mister," mingled with cries of "Good, George Bush!" and "Down Saddam!"

But reporters who crossed one of the deserted midtown bridges across the Tigris into the western area of the city discovered quickly that Mr. Hussein's hold has not been wholly broken.

Crossing the 14th of July bridge into the district of Atafiya, about five miles upriver from the Republican Palace compound that American troops seized on Monday, the reporters found themselves at least a mile north of the most advanced American positions on the west side of the river, in a neighborhood filled with angry, nervous-looking fedayeen — the irregular forces who have been among the most relentless enemies of the Americans in their 300-mile drive from Kuwait.

One reporter, lulled into a false sense of security by a day of Iraqis vilifying Mr. Hussein, approached a group of youths at an intersection to ask how they felt.

"Bush good?" the reporter asked, using the English phrase that had become the mantra of the city's eastern districts to overcome the temporary absence of an interpreter.

The youths, quickly joined by older, more threatening-looking men with Kalashnikov rifles and shoulder-holstered rockets, responded with a hostility that could have been found almost anywhere in the city until dawn today.

"Bush down shoes!" the youths answered, one of them spitting on the ground, meaning that President Bush was good only for being trampled on. "America down shoes!"

American commanders in the city barely paused to soak up the celebrations before warning tonight that much hard work remained to be done in extending the pockets of American control in east and west Baghdad into areas that remained no-man's lands, or worse, pockets of active resistance.

Those pockets were clearly still dangerous today, but they were also isolated. Many people seemed joyous. A middle-aged man pushed through a crowd attempting to topple a statue of Mr. Hussein outside the oil ministry with a bouquet of paper flowers, and passed among American troops distributing them one at a time, each with a kiss on the cheek.

A woman with two small children perched in the open roof of a car maneuvering to get close to a Marine Corps unit assisting in toppling a Hussein statue outside the Palestine and Sheraton hotels, the quarters for foreign journalists, wept as she shouted, "Thank you, mister, thank you very much."

The American breakthrough came with stunning speed, only six days after American troops gained their first foothold in Baghdad with the seizure of the city's international airport, and after many military experts had predicted it could take weeks, even months, to besiege Mr. Hussein's forces and overcome them.

The American advances that began on Tuesday night, from the southeastern edges of a city plunged into pitch darkness by the failure of the city's electricity grid, resulted by nightfall today in extending

American control over a wide southeastern quadrant of the city up to the Tigris River's eastern bank.

To this could be added the American occupation of the government quarter on the river's west bank, an area of several square miles that includes many of the principal seats of Mr. Hussein's power, including his main palaces and many government ministries, after a fierce day-long battle on Monday.

How far American troops enlarged that western foothold in a day of light skirmishing today was not clear.

On the eastern side of the river, even in no-man's areas where the American troops had not yet reached, virtually every Iraqi reporters encountered among crowds that totaled in the tens of thousands, showed disdain for Mr. Hussein.

One group of young men who marched out of Saddam City, an impoverished district that is home to perhaps two million Shiite Muslims — among the most repressed of all Mr. Hussein's victims — were asked as they dashed from one American armored vehicle to another with their handshakes and the cries of welcome why a visitor to Saddam City just a few days ago had heard only the quietest whispers of dissent.

"Because we were frightened," one young man said. "We were frightened of being killed."

A few moments earlier, another man, a 27-year-old student named Raad, had approached to voice the deep suspicions that had been sown among Iraqis by experience with previous uprisings against Mr. Hussein that had surged for a day, sometimes for a week, only to be savagely repressed.

"The question is, what happens tomorrow?" Raad, a clothing salesman, said, in faltering English. "To this moment I cannot believe we got rid of Saddam Hussein. Where is he? Is he died? We don't know it. Is he going to come back and kill us all Iraqis, to use chemical weapons? We do not know it."

One man, an official in the Oil Ministry, said flatly that any government, "Saddam Hussein or no," would be better than any imposed by the United States.

But of the main message that Iraqis wanted transmitted to the world there could be no reasonable doubt: they had yearned secretly for years to be rid of Mr. Hussein but had been too cowed to say so.

Throughout the day, there was no sign of Mr. Hussein's vaunted Republican Guard. One marine encountered at a junction on the Canal Expressway, running north to south across Baghdad's eastern outskirts, expressed his astonishment and relief. "We didn't meet a single armed Iraqi all night," he said. "They're gone. Just run right away."

Down the expressway to the south, past the abandoned United Nations headquarters and on for at least five miles, the median strip on the expressway, and a sliproad running beside, were littered with abandoned Iraqi tanks, armored personnel carriers and mobile artillery guns, most of them marked with the red triangle of the Republican Guard.

Camouflaged Iraqi uniforms and combat boots lay strewn near many of the vehicles, suggesting that the soldiers hastened into civilian clothes as they fled. Inside the tanks and armored carriers lay half-finished meals, and half-drunk cans of soda.

As with Iraqi troops, so it was with most officials who until days ago were swearing undying fealty to Mr. Hussein. The information minister, Muhammad Said al-Sahhaf, who gained a reputation earlier in the war for daily news conferences that verged on the delusional, failed to show up today at the Palestine hotel. His last words on Tuesday were: "I now inform you that you are too far from reality."

Reporters visiting the headquarters of the General Security Directorate, almost the most feared agency in Iraq until today, found its sprawling compound near the United Nations offices empty of all but a handful of looters.

As the reporters probed down corridors and into inner courtyards, they came across two heavyset men, sweating heavily, who had much of the thuggish appearance, and now the hunted look, of men who thought they might have something to answer for.

The men denied that they were officials of the directorate, which had a reputation for detaining thousands of Iraqis, and executing many of them without trial, but they refused to say what other reason they might have for being in the compound. Perhaps apprehensive that the reporters might turn them in to the Americans, they lingered, deflecting questions about the directorate and its work, all the time glancing nervously towards the gates onto the street.

When asked where the detainees were, the men said they had all fled three days ago, when American troops entered the heart of Baghdad from the west. How had they fled from locked cells? The men said they did not know. And how many detainees were there, a reporter asked. "Nobody ever knew," one man replied. "They were kept in the tunnels underground. They never saw the day."

In Saddam City, the Shiite enclave on Baghdad's northeastern rim, years of repression by Mr. Hussein, a Sunni Muslim, were thrown off today. From shortly after dawn on, word passed like wildfire through the refuse-strewn streets that every police station, every office of the ruling Baath Party, every military barracks, every outpost of the security and intelligence network, had been abandoned, many of them so fast that Mr. Hussein's loyalists had left behind Kalashnikov rifles, pistols and in some cases, even machine guns.

Saddam City, in effect, had been captured without even the Americans having to fire a shot.

Muslim clerics quickly organized an event that could not hardly have been dreamed of as late as Monday night: the re-opening of Al Mohsen mosque, the central place of worship for all Shiites in Saddam City, which was closed four years ago after Republican Guard units opened fire on demonstrators who gathered around the mosque in protesting against the killing of one of Iraq's most venerable Shiite clerics.

By lunchtime today, more than 1,000 people had gathered in and around the cool courtyard of the mosque, and crammed inside to hear the chief cleric, Sheik Amer al-Minshidawi, give the first sermon there in years from a raised wooden throne that serves as a pulpit.

His message was directed only in part at Mr. Hussein. "We have to repair everything that has been destroyed by the tyrant Saddam," he said. Then, he quickly moved on to a message for Americans.

An American Jewish scholar, he said, without giving a name, had described Islam as a "religion of terrorism." It was the duty of Shiites in Iraq, he said, now that they had been liberated by American troops, to prove that allegation wrong. "We must teach the world that Islam is a religion of peace and tolerance and love."

President Says Military Phase in Iraq Has Ended

BY DAVID E. SANGER | MAY 2, 2003

SAN DIEGO, MAY 1 — President Bush declared tonight that the military phase of the battle to topple Saddam Hussein's government was "one victory in a war on terror that began on Sept. 11th, 2001, and still goes on."

Speaking from the deck of the aircraft carrier Abraham Lincoln before thousands of uniformed sailors and aviators as the ship approached San Diego Harbor, he argued that by vanquishing Mr. Hussein's government, he had removed "an ally of Al Qaeda," and he vowed to continue to search for banned weapons in Iraq — a search that so far has been largely unsuccessful — and to confront any other nations that use such weapons to threaten the United States or could sell them to terrorists.

Mr. Bush's speech tonight, 43 days after he announced to the nation from the Oval Office that the war had begun with a surprise bombing of a compound where Mr. Hussein had been sighted, ended the combat phase of one of the swiftest wars in American military history, and one of the most dramatic chapters of Mr. Bush's presidency.

In the 20-minute speech to the men and women of the Abraham Lincoln, whose aircraft dropped nearly a third of the ordnance that rained down on Iraq, Mr. Bush made it clear that he considered the Iraq conflict just one major moment of a broader fight that he would pursue against Al Qaeda and other terrorists.

He spoke in emotional terms not only about the troops who toppled Mr. Hussein but also about the Sept. 11 attacks, melding the battle against terrorism with the battle against Iraq. "We have not forgotten the victims of Sept. 11th, the last phone calls, the cold murder of children, the searches in the rubble," he said. "With those attacks, the terrorists and their supporters declared war on the United States. And war is what they got."

The Bush administration has never linked the attacks on the World Trade Center and the Pentagon to Mr. Hussein, although senior officials did charge that Iraq had ties to the Qaeda network.

The president's stern words about governments that support terrorism and pursue illegal weapons programs appeared to be a direct warning to Iran and North Korea and "any outlaw regime that has ties to terrorist groups, and seeks or possesses weapons of mass destruction." Those states, he said, pose "a grave danger to the civilized world, and will be confronted."

Just in the last week, the State Department said Iran had the deepest ties to terrorism of any nation in the world, and North Korea boasted that it had already obtained nuclear weapons and was making more.

Mr. Bush did not declare final victory tonight as the sailors of the Lincoln, some in blue work uniforms and others in dress whites, assembled on the four-and-a-half-acre flight deck at dusk. Much remained to be done, he said, in rebuilding Iraq, and he promised that allied forces would stay as long as necessary.

White House officials said they did not want to declare a final end to the war, in part because that would require them, under the Geneva Convention, to release more than 6,000 prisoners of war, many of whom are still being interviewed.

Still, he told the sailors and fliers that "major combat operations in Iraq have ended," and that "in the battle of Iraq, the United States and our allies have prevailed."

Earlier in the day, in a visit to the carrier that the White House arranged for maximum political effect, it was hard to tell Mr. Bush from the troops he was visiting. He landed on the carrier in a Navy jet that the president, a pilot in the Texas Air National Guard three decades ago, helped pilot. The image of the president surrounded by beaming sailors was an image that White House officials clearly intend to use in the 2004 presidential campaign.

In his speech, Mr. Bush argued that the invasion and liberation of Iraq was part of the American response to the attacks of Sept. 11.

He called the tumultuous period since those attacks "19 months that changed the world," and said Mr. Hussein's defeat was a defeat for Al Qaeda and other terrorists as well.

"The liberation of Iraq is a crucial advance in the campaign against terror," he said. "We have removed an ally of Al Qaeda, and cut off a source of terrorist funding. And this much is certain: no terrorist network will gain weapons of mass destruction from the Iraqi regime, because that regime is no more."

Mr. Bush did more this evening than simply meld Mr. Hussein's fallen government with Qaeda terrorists. He both restated and amplified the "Bush doctrine," the aggressive commitment his administration has made to confront major threats before they reach American shores.

He described the attack on Iraq as an example of the extreme lengths he would go to stop such threats. "The use of force has been, and remains, our last resort," he said.

He added: "Yet all can know, friend and foe alike, that our nation has a mission: we will answer threats to our security, and we will defend the peace."

He said the mission was far from over. "Al Qaeda is wounded, not destroyed," he said, even while arguing that half of the terrorist group's senior members have been captured or killed. He vowed to pursue them "from Pakistan to the Philippines to the Horn of Africa," all places where the United States has launched counterterrorism initiatives.

Notably, Mr. Bush never once in his speech mentioned the United Nations, or the allies that opposed any use of military force, including France, Germany and Russia. His vision of the continuing war on terrorism was described as largely an American mission, to be pursued by the United States and willing partners, without reference to the international institutions set up after World War II to keep the peace. He mentioned Britain, Australia and Poland as the nations that "shared in the hardships of war." These are, in the view of many of his aides, now America's core allies, a huge shift from the main alliances in the half century since the end of the cold war.

Mr. Bush's tone was carefully measured tonight; his aides did not want him to sound too martial, or to appear to be gloating to a world that is deeply suspicious of American power. Still, he struck an optimistic and purposeful chord.

"The war on terror is not over, yet it is not endless," he said. "We do not know the day of final victory, but we have seen the turning of the tide. No act of the terrorists will change our purpose, or weaken our resolve, or alter their fate. Their cause is lost."

Mr. Bush spoke tonight nearly three weeks after the main military action — the drive from Kuwait to Baghdad — was largely completed. In perhaps the most vivid symbol of that victory, Defense Secretary Donald H. Rumsfeld, the first member of Mr. Bush's war council to visit Baghdad, used one of Mr. Hussein's former palaces as a base.

But Mr. Bush acknowledged tonight that the longer and politically more difficult task of remaking Iraq was only in its opening phase.

"The transition from dictatorship to democracy will take time, but it is worth every effort," he said. Then, the man who was elected president on a platform that called for reducing the use of the American military to conduct what he called "nation building" made it clear that the military would be the central participant in that effort.

"Our coalition will stay until our work is done," he said.

While Mr. Bush used his visit to the Lincoln to all but declare victory, two of the major objectives of the war — capturing Mr. Hussein and finding banned weapons — remain unfulfilled. Already, both are lingering irritants to the administration.

In an interview this week, a senior administration official who was deeply involved in all aspects of planning and executing the war said many members of Mr. Bush's inner circle believed that Mr. Hussein was dead, although they were frustrated that they could not prove it.

Referring to the two bombing raids on residences that Mr. Hussein was believed to be visiting — one on the opening night of the war, another toward the last days of heavy battle in Baghdad — the senior official said, "I think there is a good chance that we got him one of those times, but I don't know for certain."

The official cautioned against "equating this for the hunt for Osama bin Laden."

"We've all fallen into a trap on this," the official contended, making an argument that Mr. Bush himself has made in private, according to those who have spoken with him.

"This is somebody who ruled by traditional means of power: terror, an army, Republican Guard, territory, weapons, wealth, the ability to threaten his neighbors, like Adolf Hitler did and Joseph Stalin did. Without those traditional means he's got nothing."

The official noted that "we did not know what happened to Adolf Hitler for certain — until 1971. But did anybody think Hitler was still in power?"

Still, other members of the administration are clearly concerned that until Mr. Hussein is proved dead, his loyalists will still harass American occupation troops, setting off grenade attacks or car bombs.

"It's a problem," one senior military official said early this week. "There's a great desire to prove he is no longer among us."

Politically more complex for the administration is the continuing search for chemical and biological weapons, a search that so far has turned up next to nothing. One member of Mr. Bush's war cabinet said that he suspected that Mr. Hussein had not mounted his chemical stockpiles on weapons, but suggested that sooner or later they would be found. Mr. Bush himself said tonight that the United States knew of "hundreds of sites that will be investigated."

One senior administration official said, however, that the White House was now "learning something important on how the Iraqis did this."

"What you are likely to see is not large stockpiles of weapons of mass destruction but all of the elements, the precursors, the capacity to put them together quickly." The official speculated that Mr. Hussein "got caught in a trap of his own making."

"He couldn't put them together as long as the inspections were going on" before to the war, he said.

"The inspections went up to very close to the time of hostility. Was it then too late to begin to try to assemble these things? Did he try to destroy them to cover the evidence?" The key, the aide said, was interviewing scientists in the environment of a newly liberated Iraq, "where they might say something."

The Failure to Find Iraqi Weapons

OPINION | BY THE NEW YORK TIMES | SEPT. 26, 2003

THIS PAGE DID NOT support the war in Iraq, but it never quarreled with one of its basic premises. Like President Bush, we believed that Saddam Hussein was hiding potentially large quantities of chemical and biological weapons and aggressively pursuing nuclear arms. Like the president, we thought those weapons posed a grave danger to the United States and the rest of the world. Now it appears that premise was wrong. We cannot in hindsight blame the administration for its original conclusions. They were based on the best intelligence available, which had led the Clinton administration before it and the governments of allied nations to reach the same conclusion. But even the best intelligence can turn out to be mistaken, and the likelihood that this was the case in Iraq shows why pre-emptive war, the Bush administration's strategy since 9/11, is so ill conceived as a foundation for security policy. If intelligence and risk assessment are sketchy — and when are they not? — using them as the basis for pre-emptive war poses enormous dangers.

A draft of an interim report by David Kay, the American leading the hunt for banned arms in Iraq, says the team has not found any such weapons after nearly four months of intensively searching and interviewing top Iraqi scientists. There is some evidence of chemicals and equipment that could have been put to illicit use. But, to the chagrin of Mr. Bush's top lieutenants, there is nothing more.

It remains remotely possible, of course, that something will be found. But Mr. Kay's draft suggests that the weapons are simply not there. Why Mr. Hussein did not prove that when the United Nations demanded an explanation remains a puzzle. His failure to come clean strengthened the conviction that he had a great deal to hide. His history as a vicious tyrant who had used chemical weapons in war and against his own people lent credence to the fear that he could not be trusted with whatever he was holding and would pose a significant threat.

Before the war, we objected not to the stated goal of disarming Iraq but to the fact that the United States was waging war essentially alone, in defiance of many important allies. We favored using international inspectors to keep Iraq's destructive programs in check while diplomats forged a United Nations effort to force Mr. Hussein to yield his weapons.

The policy of pre-emption that Mr. Bush pursued instead junked an approach that had served this country and the world well for half a century. That policy, simply stated, was that the United States would respond quickly to aggression but would not be the first to attack.

The world changed on Sept. 11, 2001. Terrorist groups like Al Qaeda are dedicated to inflicting maximum harm on this country. Since such groups rely on suicide bombers and are therefore immune to threats of retaliation, the United States is right to attack a terrorist group first in some circumstances. It was certainly justified in its war in Afghanistan, which had become little more than a government-sponsored training camp for Al Qaeda. It is quite another thing, however, to launch a pre-emptive military campaign against a nation that the United States suspects poses a threat.

Americans and others in the world are glad that Mr. Hussein has been removed from power. If Iraq can be turned into a freer and happier country in coming years, it could become a focal point for the evolution of a more peaceful and democratic Middle East. But it was the fear of weapons of mass destruction placed in the hands of enemy terrorists that made doing something about Iraq seem urgent. If it had seemed unlikely that Mr. Hussein had them, we doubt that Congress or the American people would have endorsed the war.

This is clearly an uncomfortable question for the Bush administration. Yesterday, Secretary of State Colin Powell met with Times editors. Asked whether Americans would have supported this war if weapons of mass destruction had not been at issue, Mr. Powell said the question was too hypothetical to answer. Asked if he, personally, would have supported it, he smiled, thrust his hand out and said, "It was good to meet you."

A Shifting Enemy: U.S. Generals Say Civil War, Not Insurgency, Is Greatest Threat

BY MARK MAZZETTI | NOV. 18, 2006

WASHINGTON, NOV. 17 — In the fall of 2005, the generals running the Iraq war told the Senate Armed Services Committee that a gradual withdrawal of American troops from Iraq was imperative.

The American troop presence, Gen. John P. Abizaid and Gen. George W. Casey Jr. said at the time, was stoking the insurgency, fostering dependency among the Iraqi security forces and proving counterproductive for what General Abizaid has called "The Long War" against Islamic radicalism.

This week, General Abizaid, chief of the United States Central Command, told the same committee that American forces may be all that is preventing full-scale civil war in Iraq, so a phased troop withdrawal would be a mistake. What has changed, military experts and intelligence officials say, is that the insurgency of Baathists and foreign jihadists is no longer the greatest enemy the United States faces in Iraq. The biggest danger now, they say, is that violence between Shiites and Sunnis could destroy Iraq's government and spill across the Middle East.

General Abizaid and other American commanders may continue to worry about the long-term consequences of keeping an American occupation force of more than 100,000 troops in an Arab country indefinitely.

But in his testimony to Congress on Wednesday, General Abizaid made it clear that he thought he had no option but to focus on the most immediate threat, the sectarian violence threatening to split Iraq apart.

The Pentagon, which long ago discarded the idea that it would be American troops that would defeat the Iraqi insurgency, has made the training of Iraqi security forces its primary mission in Iraq. But Iraqi forces are still far from capable of quashing sectarian violence, and that is the principal reason that American commanders say they believe that a substantial American troop presence is still needed.

On Wednesday, General Abizaid announced a plan to bulk up the number of trainers embedded with Iraqi troops, but few military experts believe that the capacity of Iraqi troops is likely to improve so much that a significant American troop reduction would be prudent in the short run.

"While it would make a great deal of sense to progressively turn things over to the Iraqis and reduce our presence, it is no more practical in the fall of 2006 than it was in the fall of 2005, and that's the worrisome part," said Andrew F. Krepinevich Jr., a counterinsurgency expert and the executive director of the Center for Strategic and Budgetary Assessments.

Last fall, General Casey told the Senate that it was essential to cut the American presence in Iraq as a way of pushing more Iraqi troops onto the frontlines and reducing "dependency." As late as this summer, he had been drawing up plans for a troop drawdown that would drastically cut the American presence in Iraq by the end of next year.

But these days, troop levels in Iraq are going up, rather than down.

A unit of about 2,200 marines that had been aboard naval warships in the Persian Gulf has begun moving into Anbar Province, the restive Sunni stronghold west of Baghdad. Some in the Pentagon have worried that Anbar Province — which includes the violent cities of Falluja and Ramadi — is particularly vulnerable with the American military currently focused on an offensive to secure the most violent neighborhoods of Baghdad, the capital.

On Friday, the Pentagon also announced a new set of deployment orders for troops that will enter Iraq early in 2007, most for yearlong combat tours.

American commanders had hoped by this point to be deploying fewer combat brigades into Iraq than the number rotating out, but the

Pentagon is now planning to keep a base level of about 141,000 troops in the country, with the possibility of "surging" more troops as needed.

In his own testimony before the Senate Armed Services Committee, Gen. Michael V. Hayden, director of the Central Intelligence Agency, described how the spiraling violence would create new difficulties for American forces, whether in Baghdad or Falluja.

"The longer this goes on, the less controlled the violence is, the more the violence devolves down to the neighborhood level," he said. "The center disappears, and normal people acting not irrationally end up acting like extremists."

For his part, General Abizaid insisted that every commander running the Iraq war believed that the mission could ultimately succeed.

"It's not a matter of personal pride," he said. "It's a matter of seeing that the enemy can't win."

General Abizaid, who has spoken eloquently in the past about what could be a decades long fight against Islamic radicalism, is also well aware that keeping such high troop levels in Iraq could also be the catalyst for a new generation of radicals committed to jihad.

Appearing shortly after General Abizaid, General Hayden said that the American presence in Iraq "gives life to Al Qaeda propaganda that they misuse and misrepresent to the larger Arab world."

Pointedly, General Hayden declined repeatedly to characterize Iraq as "the central battlefront in the war on terror," as senior Bush administration officials have described it.

Under questioning from Senator Lindsey Graham, Republican of South Carolina, he referred to Iraq instead as an "absolutely critical battlefront."

THOM SHANKER CONTRIBUTED REPORTING.

A Matter of Definition: What Makes a Civil War, and Who Declares It So?

BY EDWARD WONG | NOV. 26, 2006

BAGHDAD, NOV. 25 — Is Iraq in a civil war?

Though the Bush administration continues to insist that it is not, a growing number of American and Iraqi scholars, leaders and policy analysts say the fighting in Iraq meets the standard definition of civil war.

The common scholarly definition has two main criteria. The first says that the warring groups must be from the same country and fighting for control of the political center, control over a separatist state or to force a major change in policy. The second says that at least 1,000 people must have been killed in total, with at least 100 from each side.

American professors who specialize in the study of civil wars say that most of their number are in agreement that Iraq's conflict is a civil war.

"I think that at this time, and for some time now, the level of violence in Iraq meets the definition of civil war that any reasonable person would have," said James Fearon, a political scientist at Stanford.

While the term is broad enough to include many kinds of conflicts, one of the sides in a civil war is almost always a sovereign government. So some scholars now say civil war began when the Americans transferred sovereignty to an appointed Iraqi government in June 2004. That officially transformed the anti-American war into one of insurgent groups seeking to regain power for disenfranchised Sunni Arabs against an Iraqi government led by Prime Minister Ayad Allawi and increasingly dominated by Shiites.

Others say the civil war began this year, after the bombing of a revered Shiite shrine in Samarra set off a chain of revenge killings that left hundreds dead over five days and has yet to end. Mr. Allawi proclaimed a month after that bombing that Iraq was mired in a civil war. "If this is not civil war, then God knows what civil war is," he said.

Many insurgencies and ethnic or sectarian wars are also civil wars. Vietnam and Lebanon are examples. Scholars say the Iraq civil war has elements of both an insurgency — one side is struggling to topple what it sees as an illegitimate national government — and a sectarian war — the besieged government is ruled by Shiites and opposed by Sunni Arabs.

In Iraq, sectarian purges and Sunni-Shiite revenge killings have become a hallmark of the fighting, but the cycles of violence are ignited by militia leaders who have political goals. The former Yugoslav president, Slobodan Milosovic, did this during the wars in the Balkans.

The civil strife in Iraq largely takes place in mixed Sunni-Shiite areas that include the cities of Baghdad, Mosul and Baquba. In Anbar Province, which is overwhelming Sunni Arab, much of the violence is aimed at American troops. Large swaths of Iraq have little violence, but those areas are relatively homogenous and have few people.

Governments and people embroiled in a civil war often do not want to label it as such. In Colombia, officials insisted for years that the rebels there were merely bandits.

Some Bush administration officials have argued that there is no obvious political vision on the part of the Sunni-led insurgent groups, so "civil war" does not apply.

In the United States, the debate over the term rages because many politicians, especially those who support the war, believe there would be domestic political implications to declaring it a civil war. They fear that an acknowledgment by the White House and its allies would be seen as an admission of a failure of President Bush's Iraq policy.

They also worry that the American people might not see a role for American troops in an Iraqi civil war and would more loudly demand a withdrawal.

But in fact, many scholars say the bloodshed here already puts Iraq in the top ranks of the civil wars of the last half-century. The carnage of recent days — beginning with bombings on Thursday in a Shiite district of Baghdad that killed more than 200 people — reinforces their assertion.

Mr. Fearon and a colleague at Stanford, David D. Laitin, say the deaths per year in Iraq, with at least 50,000 reportedly killed since March 2003, place this conflict on par with wars in Burundi and Bosnia.

Iraq's president and prime minister avoid using the term, but many Iraqis say extremists have thrust the country into civil war, even as moderates have struggled to pull back from the brink.

"You need to let the world know there's a civil war here in Iraq," said Adel Ibrahim, 44, a sheik in the Subiah tribe, which is mostly Shiite. "It's a crushing civil war. Mortars kill children in our neighborhoods. We're afraid to travel anywhere because we'll be killed in buses. We don't know who is our enemy and who is our friend."

The spiraling bloodshed here bolsters arguments that this is a civil war. A United Nations report released Wednesday said at least 3,709 Iraqis were killed in October, the highest of any month since the American-led invasion. More than 100,000 Iraqis a month are fleeing to Syria and Jordan.

"It's stunning; it should have been called a civil war a long time ago, but now I don't see how people can avoid calling it a civil war," said Nicholas Sambanis, a political scientist at Yale who co-edited "Understanding Civil War: Evidence and Analysis," published by the World Bank in 2005. "The level of violence is so extreme that it far surpasses most civil wars since 1945."

Among scholars, "there's a consensus," Mr. Sambanis said. Scholars in the United States generally agree that there have been at least 100 civil wars since 1945. At the smaller end of the scale is the war in Northern Ireland. Measured by total killed, the largest modern civil wars were in Angola, Afghanistan, Nigeria, China and Rwanda.

However, there are some dissenting historians on the definition of civil war, and whether it applies to Iraq. John Keegan, the British writer of war histories, finds only five clear-cut cases, starting with the English civil war of the 17th century through to the Lebanese war of the 20th century. His criteria are that the feuding groups must be vying for national authority, have leaders who publicly announce what they are fighting for and clash in set-piece battles while wearing uniforms, among other things. He argues in the December issue of Prospect magazine that Iraq is therefore not in civil war.

On Friday, Scott Stanzel, a White House spokesman, insisted that the Iraq conflict was not civil war, noting that Iraq's top leaders had agreed with that assessment. Last month, Tony Snow, the chief spokesman for President Bush, acknowledged that there were many groups trying to undermine the government, but said that there was no civil war because "it's not clear that they are operating as a unified force. You don't have a clearly identifiable leader."

By contrast, Sen. Joseph R. Biden Jr., the top Democrat on the Senate Foreign Relations Committee, said on Fox News in September that "a political solution is necessary to end the civil war in Iraq."

In 2003, at the start of the Sunni-led insurgency, Bush administration officials called the guerrillas "dead-enders" and insisted their only goal was to sow chaos. Now, American commanders acknowledge that political dominance is at the heart of this conflict.

In Congressional testimony this month, Lt. Gen. Michael D. Maples of the Defense Intelligence Agency characterized the situation as an "ongoing, violent struggle for power" and said the country was moving closer to a "significant breakdown of central authority."

Many Iraqis and Americans who have tracked the insurgency say it has been strongly shaped by former Baath Party members who want to keep Shiites from taking power. Even the newer jihadist groups have articulated political goals on Web sites — most notably to establish a Sunni-ruled Islamic caliphate.

"There was a whole regime that ruled this country for 35 years," said Mahmoud Othman, a senior Kurdish legislator. "Now they've gone underground. This is the main body of the resistance."

Scholars say it is crucial that policy makers and news media organizations recognize the Iraq conflict as a civil war.

"Why should we care how it is defined, if we all agree that the violence is unacceptable?" asked Mr. Laitin, the Stanford professor. "Here is my answer: There is a scientific community that studies civil wars, and understands their dynamics and how they, in general, end. This research is valuable to our nation's security."

REPORTING WAS CONTRIBUTED BY QAIS MIZHER FROM BAGHDAD, AND BY MARK MAZZETTI, JIM RUTENBERG AND KATE ZERNIKE FROM WASHINGTON.

3,000 Deaths in Iraq, Countless Tears at Home

BY LIZETTE ALVAREZ AND ANDREW LEHREN | JAN. 1, 2007

JORDAN W. HESS was the unlikeliest of soldiers.

He could bench-press 300 pounds and then go home and write poetry. He learned the art of glass blowing because it seemed interesting and built a computer with only a magazine as his guide. Most recently, he fell in love with a woman from Brazil and took up digital photography, letting both sweep his heart away.

Specialist Hess, the seventh of eight children, was never keen on premonitions, but on Christmas of 2005, as his tight-knit family gathered on a beach for the weekend, he told each sibling and parent privately that he did not expect to come home from Iraq.

On Nov. 11, Specialist Hess, 26, freshly arrived in Iraq, was conducting a mission as the driver of an Abrams tank when an improvised explosive device, or I.E.D., blew up with brain-rattling force. The blast was so potent it penetrated the 67-ton tank, flinging him against the top and critically injuring his spine. His three crewmates survived. For three weeks, he hung on at Brooke Army Medical Center in San Antonio, long enough to utter a few words to his loved ones and absorb their kindness.

On Dec. 4, Specialist Hess slipped onto the ever-expanding list of American military fatalities in Iraq, one that has increased by an average of more than three a day since Oct. 1, the highest three-month toll in two years. On Sunday, with the announcement of the death in Baghdad of Specialist Dustin R. Donica, 22, of Spring, Tex., the list reached the somber milestone of at least 3,000 deaths since the March 2003 invasion.

The landmark reflects how much more dangerous and muddled a soldier's job in Iraq has become in the face of a growing and increasingly sophisticated insurgency. Violence in the country is at an all-time

The grave of Gunnery Sgt. John D. Fry, 28, in Waco, Tex. He leaves a wife and three children.

high, according to a Pentagon report released last month. December was the third deadliest month for American troops since the start of the war, with insurgents claiming 111 soldiers' lives. October and November also witnessed a high number of casualties, 106 and 68 respectively, as American forces stepped up combat operations to try to stabilize Baghdad.

"It escalated while I was there," said Capt. Scott Stanford, a National Guard officer who was a commander of a headquarters company in Ramadi for a year, arriving in June 2005. "When we left this June, it was completely unhinged. There was a huge increase in the suicide car bombs we had. The I.E.D.'s were bigger and more complex."

"And it was very tense before we left in terms of snipers," said Captain Stanford, a member of the Iraq and Afghanistan Veterans of America. "I don't know if there were more of them, or if they were getting better."

This spike in violence, which has been felt most profoundly by Iraqi civilians, who are dying by the thousands, has stoked feverish debate about the nation's presence in Iraq. Many Democrats in Congress are urging a phased withdrawal from the country, and the Bush administration is leaning toward deploying additional troops in 2007. If the conflict continues into March, the Iraq war will be the third longest in American history, ranked behind the Vietnam War and the American Revolution.

President Bush did not specifically acknowledge reaching the milestone of 3,000 American deaths, but a White House spokesman, Scott Stanzel, said the president "grieves for each one that is lost" and would ensure that their sacrifices were not made in vain. The campaign against terrorism, Mr. Stanzel said, will be a long struggle.

Specialist Hess had volunteered for his mission to spare another soldier the danger of going outside the wire that day. Like so many of his fallen comrades, he had become the victim of an inescapably dangerous roadside landscape.

"It was the type of injury you rarely recover from; in past wars you wouldn't have gotten out of theater," said his father, Bill Hess, a Boeing engineer and retired Air Force man. "So that was a blessing, that he could talk to us. He mouthed words and we were able to say we loved him. There is a lot to be said for that."

A STEADY TOLL OF DEATHS

In many ways, the third 1,000 men and women to die in Iraq faced the same unflinching challenge as the second 1,000 soldiers to die there — a dedicated and ruthless Iraqi insurgency that has exploited the power of roadside bombs to chilling effect. These bombs now cause about half of all American combat deaths and injuries in Iraq.

Over all, the casualty rate has remained relatively steady since 2005, dipping only slightly. It took 14 months for the death toll to jump to 2,000 soldiers from 1,000. It took about two weeks longer for it to rise to 3,000 from 2,000, during the period covering Oct. 25, 2005, to this week.

Dawn Bowman, 26, at the grave of her husband, Lance Cpl. Jon Eric Bowman, 21, in Shane, La. Three days before he redeployed to Iraq in September, he told her he was having dreams that he wouldn't return home.

"It is hugely frustrating, tragic and disappointing that we can't reduce the fatality rate," said Michael O'Hanlon, a military analyst for the Brookings Institution.

The service members who died during this latest period fit an unchanging profile. They were mostly white men from rural areas, soldiers so young they still held fresh memories of high school football heroics and teenage escapades. Many men and women were in Iraq for the second or third time. Some were going on their fourth, fifth or sixth deployment.

But in other ways, the situation has changed in the past year. Improvised explosive devices — the kind that killed Specialist Hess — have grown deadlier, despite concerted Pentagon efforts and billions of dollars spent trying to counteract them. Insurgents are now more adept at concealing bombs, booby-trapping them and powering them to penetrate well-armored vehicles. They are also scattering more of them along countless roads using myriad triggers and hiding spots — under garbage and tires, behind guardrails, inside craters.

At the same time, Iraqi citizens have grown less inclined to tip off soldiers to the presence of these bombs. About 1,200 roadside bombs were detonated in August.

The toll of war has fallen most heavily this year on regular Army soldiers, at least 544 of whom died in this group of 1,000, compared with 405 in the last group. This increase was the result of fewer National Guard soldiers and reservists being deployed to Iraq in 2006.

Considering the intensity of the violence in Iraq this year, it is remarkable that the casualty rate did not climb higher, analysts and officers say. Long-awaited improvements in body and vehicle armor have helped protect soldiers, and advances in battlefield medicine have saved many lives. New procedures, like leaving wounds open to prevent infection, and relaying soldiers to hospitals faster than ever, have kept more service members alive. Troops now carry their own tourniquets.

During World War II, 30 percent of all wounded soldiers died of their injuries, a number that dipped to 24 percent during the Vietnam War and then to 9 percent for the Iraq conflict. Though this is a positive development, it also means that more soldiers are coming home with life-changing injuries, including amputations and brain trauma. More than 22,000 soldiers have been wounded in Iraq.

"There is no question that the number of dead should have been far higher," said Dr. William Winkenwerder, the assistant secretary of defense for health affairs, referring to the Iraqi conflict. "Some of these blast injuries are very powerful."

Bombs and bullets are not the only things that can kill soldiers; nearly 20 percent of those who die in Iraq do so outside of combat operations. Sometimes it is the hazard of driving too quickly on badly rutted roads to avoid danger. Humvees, weighted down with armor, can easily flip if maneuvered too quickly. Many of Iraq's roads are not built to hold heavy vehicles, and the ground can give way, tossing multi-ton machines into narrow canals where soldiers have drowned. Helicopters are sometimes strafed by sandstorms or crippled by mechanical malfunctions. Accidents make up two-thirds of the nonhostile deaths.

With so many soldiers carrying so many weapons, unintentional casualties occur, sometimes while handling firearms. Fire from one's own side is another inevitability of war, as is suicide. Since March 2003, 93 soldiers have died from self-inflicted wounds in Iraq.

In a way, these deaths, coming not at the hands of the enemy, but as a consequence of inferior roads and turbulent weather, can be even more difficult for parents to accept. Sometimes they wait months for official reports, since all noncombat deaths must be investigated.

"I don't think I ever thought something like this could happen," said Shelley Burnett, whose son, Lance Cpl. Jason K. Burnett, 20, died in May after his tank toppled into a canal. "We talked a lot about the I.E.D.'s and the dangers out there, but Jason kept saying, 'There is not a whole lot they can do to a tank.' "

DEATH AT ROADSIDE

Over the last two years, the Pentagon has worked frantically to harden body armor and the armor on its Humvees and other vehicles. And the insurgents in Iraq have responded just as forcefully with deadly innovations in roadside bombs, and a fury of sniper bullets.

The most lethal development is the use of the "explosively formed penetrators," which pierce armor and stay intact when they explode. Roadside bombs are often detonated from a distance — with garage door openers, for example — or automatically, from pressure-sensitive devices, like a simple rubber air hose. Motion detectors and infrared devices are also used.

The vast majority of these bombs do not kill soldiers, or even injure them seriously. Four out of five I.E.D.'s that detonate do not cause casualties, an improvement over previous years, the Pentagon says. But those devices that do cause casualties are killing more soldiers. An analysis by The New York Times of military records found that in 2003, the devices accounted for 16 percent of troop fatalities. This year, they accounted for 43 percent. And an increasing number are killing more than one soldier.

"Unfortunately, when there is a fatal I.E.D. attack, there often are multiple wounded and casualties," said Christine DeVries, a spokeswoman for the Pentagon's Joint I.E.D. Defeat Organization. "The enemy has had some success in adapting to what we are doing."

Lance Cpl. Jon Eric Bowman, 21, affectionate and angel-faced, was typical of many of the soldiers and marines who found their calling in the military. He was raised in rural Dubach, La., far from the razzmatazz of New Orleans, and could not wait to join after the Sept. 11 attacks.

He was first sent to Iraq early in 2005. When he came home later that year, he had changed. Three days before he was set to redeploy this September, he sat with his wife in their truck and talked for six hours.

"He was crying, he was so scared," said his wife, Dawn Bowman, 26. "He was having dreams that he wasn't coming back."

In fact, Corporal Bowman had been having blackouts, migraines and a tic, new ailments from his time in Iraq, his wife said. The diagnosis was Tourette's syndrome, and he was then told by doctors in in Louisiana that fluid had built up in his brain.

He wound up back in Iraq, anyway. "They felt he was just trying to get out of Iraq," said Johnny Bowman, the corporal's father, of his son's superiors. "That there was really nothing wrong with him. That's what he told me on the phone."

Corporal Bowman did not push the issue, feeling guilty about abandoning his fellow marines. On Oct. 9, his Humvee ran across a roadside bomb, killing him instantly. He had been manning the machine gun.

"Jon Eric was not just my only son," his father said. "He was my best friend."

Lance Cpl. Jeromy D. West, 20, a mortar man who loved to fish as much as he hated to study, was killed on Nov. 25 by a sniper bullet as he stood guard on a roof in Haditha. It was his second deployment.

In December, shortly after word of his death, his family honored his wishes and held a memorial for him on the football field at Hamilton

High School, near San Diego, where he had been a star player. A thousand people showed up.

"Everybody liked him," his stepfather, Ron Klopf, said. "People would say, 'God, your son is polite.' And I would say, 'My kid?' I called him Eddie Haskell — so polite at everybody else's house."

Corporal West was goofy in the best way. Not long before he joined the Marines, he and his friend would compete to see who could get a bigger freeze headache from eating too much ice cream. They would writhe in pain. Then they would do it again. He was 17 when he decided to get serious and join the corps, something his parents tried to talk him out of.

" 'You can get killed doing this,' " Mr. Klopf remembers saying. "And he said, 'Should we send some other parent's kid out there?' And that's how he was."

For Corporal Burnett, death came not from bullets or bombs but from riding in a tank in a country crisscrossed with irrigation canals and crumbly roads. Just two years after graduating from high school in St. Cloud, Fla., where he spent his summers building houses for the poor and four-wheeling on back-country roads, Corporal Burnett's tank fell off a bridge and plunged into a canal, in which he drowned.

His mother cannot forget the day Jason and his younger brother tossed her back and forth in the yard to make her scream with laughter. "He was a fun-loving kid," Mrs. Burnett said. "If you heard laughter, you knew Jason was around."

Optimism was Specialist Robert F. Weber's indelible quality. A gunner from Cincinnati, he had warned his mother, Cathy, that the roads in Iraq were wretched. She worried a lot during his first deployment, particularly after he sent home a roll of film to develop. The first print she saw was of a missile hitting a barracks.

But he made it back to America and bought a blue Kia, the color of his eyes, before redeploying three weeks later. The Army had been a good fit. "He was proud of himself," she said of Bobby, her only child. "I was very proud. It was like he found his niche."

On his second deployment, though, the situation in Iraq had become grimmer. "Mom, things are getting worse over here, more dangerous," he said, from his base near Mosul the Saturday before he died. "The roads are bad. You don't run over anything even if it looks like a piece of paper."

But the lumbering armored Humvee he was on never hit a bomb on Sept. 30. It swerved somehow and flipped, killing him.

Mrs. Weber said she cannot imagine seeing the troops walk away from Iraq now, when democracy seems as unattainable as ever. "For what did all these guys get killed over there?" she asked, incredulously. "What for?"

SEVEN DAYS FROM HOME

Back in America, countless families and friends have waited and worried and tried their best these past years to keep themselves busy until their husbands, sons, wives, daughters, fathers, mothers or buddies returned home safely. For 3,000 of them, the reunion never came.

In too many cases, the homecoming was tantalizingly near, a few more X's on the calendar and the vigil would be over. A number of soldiers were killed just days and weeks from the end of their deployment, a date close enough to allow those back home to lower their guard a trifle, making the deaths all the more devastating.

"It's almost like Christmas is here, and you wake up Christmas morning and there is no Christmas," said Col. Bill Rochelle, a retired National Guard commander of the 42nd Division support command.

Gunnery Sgt. John D. Fry, a 28-year-old marine from Lorena, Tex., was seven days from scooping up his wife, Malia, and his three kids into a group hug back in America. "My plans," Sergeant Fry told his commander, "are to go home and wrestle with my kids."

He and Mrs. Fry were only 15 when they went on their first date, to see "A League of Their Own," and then to eat ice cream at the mall. Mom and Dad drove them home. A year later, he plopped her on his lap and proposed. They kept their engagement a secret. Not long after, he was named salutatorian at Heritage Christian Academy. Another student bested him for the top title; it was the future Mrs. Fry, the valedictorian.

"We were soul mates," Mrs. Fry said. On Nov. 15, 1995, five days after he graduated from boot camp, they were married.

Mr. Fry, who liked a challenge, specialized in defusing explosive devices, a nerve-racking skill he brought with him to Iraq. "Babe," Mrs. Fry recalled his saying when he chose the specialty, "it's dangerous, but I want to do it. And I said, 'Let's go.' "

A team leader, Sergeant Fry, who shipped out to Iraq in September 2005, disarmed 73 bombs, including one of the biggest car bombs found in Falluja. Once he helped defuse a suicide vest that insurgents had belted to a mentally handicapped Iraqi teenage boy. The boy had been beaten and chained to a wall. Another time, he spotted a bomb from the roof of a house. A little boy popped into the yard, hovering dangerously close to it. Sergeant Fry won his confidence by playing peekaboo, then got him to move away.

He was in "very high spirits" in March, calling his wife to say that his duties were done, his paperwork filed and his anticipation impossible to stifle. "He had made it," she said. Then a mission came down, and commanders were preparing to send a team of mostly inexperienced men to defuse bombs along a road in Al Anbar province. He volunteered for the job, instead. "That is how he led," Mrs. Fry said.

Sergeant Fry found three bombs that night and defused them. But the insurgents had hidden a fourth bomb under the third one, a booby-trap. It blew up and killed him. An Army team stayed with his body for six hours, fending off enemy fire in the dark until soldiers with mortuary affairs arrived to take his body away.

The war never scared him, Mrs. Fry said.

"It was hard, but he felt he was making a difference," she said. "He believed truly, that if he wasn't over there, they would be trying to harm us here."

MARK MAZZETTI AND GRIFF PALMER CONTRIBUTED REPORTING.

Obama Declares an End to Combat Mission in Iraq

BY HELENE COOPER AND SHERYL GAY STOLBERG | AUG. 31, 2010

WASHINGTON — President Obama declared an end on Tuesday to the seven-year American combat mission in Iraq, saying that the United States has met its responsibility to that country and that it is now time to turn to pressing problems at home.

In a prime-time address from the Oval Office, Mr. Obama balanced praise for the troops who fought and died in Iraq with his conviction that getting into the conflict had been a mistake in the first place. But he also used the moment to emphasize that he sees his primary job as addressing the weak economy and other domestic issues — and to make clear that he intends to begin disengaging from the war in Afghanistan next summer.

"We have sent our young men and women to make enormous sacrifices in Iraq, and spent vast resources abroad at a time of tight budgets at home," Mr. Obama said. "Through this remarkable chapter in the history of the United States and Iraq, we have met our responsibility. Now, it's time to turn the page."

Seeking to temper partisan feelings over the war on a day when Republicans pointed out that Mr. Obama had opposed the troop surge generally credited with helping to bring Iraq a measure of stability, the president offered some praise for his predecessor, George W. Bush. Mr. Obama acknowledged their disagreement over Iraq but said that no one could doubt Mr. Bush's "support for our troops, or his love of country and commitment to our security."

Mr. Obama spoke for about 18 minutes, saying that violence would continue in Iraq and that the United States would continue to play a key role in nurturing a stable democracy there. He celebrated America's fighting forces as "the steel in our ship of state," and pledged not to waver in the fight against Al Qaeda.

President Obama addressed the nation from the Oval Office about the end of combat in Iraq on Tuesday night.

But he suggested that he sees his role in addressing domestic issues as dominant, saying that it would be difficult to get the economy rolling again but that doing so was "our central mission as a people, and my central responsibility as president."

With his party facing the prospect of losing control of Congress in this fall's elections and his own poll numbers depressed in large part because of the lackluster economy and still-high unemployment, he said the nation's perseverance in Iraq must be matched by determination to address problems at home.

Over the last decade, "we have spent over a trillion dollars at war, often financed by borrowing from overseas," he said. "And so at this moment, as we wind down the war in Iraq, we must tackle those challenges at home with as much energy and grit and sense of common purpose as our men and women in uniform who have served abroad."

Mr. Obama acknowledged a war fatigue among Americans who have called into question his focus on the Afghanistan war, now approaching its 10th year. He said that American forces in Afghanistan "will be in place for a limited time" to give Afghans the chance to build their government and armed forces.

"But, as was the case in Iraq, we cannot do for Afghans what they must ultimately do for themselves," the president said. He reiterated that next July he would begin transferring responsibility for security to Afghans, at a pace to be determined by conditions.

"But make no mistake: this transition will begin, because open-ended war serves neither our interests nor the Afghan people's," he said.

This was no iconic end-of-war moment with photos of soldiers kissing nurses in Times Square or victory parades down America's Main Streets.

Instead, in the days leading to the Tuesday night deadline for the withdrawal of American combat troops, it has appeared as if administration officials and the American military were the only ones marking the end of this country's combat foray into Iraq. Vice President Joseph R. Biden Jr., and Adm. Mike Mullen, the chairman of the Joint Chiefs of Staff, are all in Baghdad for the official ceremony on Wednesday.

The very sight of Mr. Obama addressing Americans from the Oval Office — from the same desk where Mr. Bush announced the beginning of the conflict — shows the distance traveled since the Iraq war began. On the night of March 20, 2003, when the Army's Third Infantry Division first rolled over the border from Kuwait into Iraq, Mr. Obama was a state senator in Illinois.

Mr. Bush was at the height of his popularity, and the perception at home and in many places abroad was that America could achieve its national security goals primarily through military power. One of the biggest fears among the American troops in the convoy pouring into Iraq that night — every one of them suited in gas masks and wearing biohazard suits — was that the man they came to topple might unleash a chemical weapons attack.

Seven years and five months later, the biggest fears of American soldiers revolve around the primitive, basic, homemade bombs and old explosives in Afghanistan that were left over from the Soviet invasion. In Iraq, what was perceived as a threat from a powerful dictator, Saddam Hussein, has dissolved into the worry that as United States troops pull out they are leaving behind an unstable and weak government that could be influenced by Iran.

On Tuesday, a senior intelligence official said that Iran continues to supply militant groups in Iraq with weapons, training and equipment.

"Much has changed since that night," when Mr. Bush announced the war in Iraq, Mr. Obama said. "A war to disarm a state became a fight against an insurgency. Terrorism and sectarian warfare threatened to tear Iraq apart. Thousands of Americans gave their lives; tens of thousands have been wounded. Our relations abroad were strained. Our unity at home was tested."

The withdrawal of combat forces represents a significant milestone after the war that toppled Mr. Hussein, touched off waves of sectarian strife and claimed the lives of more than 4,400 American soldiers and more than 70,000 Iraqis, according to United States and Iraqi government figures.

"Operation Iraqi Freedom is over," Mr. Obama said, using the military name for the mission, "and the Iraqi people now have lead responsibility for the security of their country."

As Mr. Obama prepared to observe the end of one phase of the war, he called Mr. Bush from Air Force One, as he was en route to Fort Bliss in Texas to meet with American troops home from Iraq.

The two spoke "just for a few moments," Ben Rhodes, deputy national security adviser for strategic communications, told reporters aboard the plane, declining to give any additional details.

American troops reached Mr. Obama's goal for the drawdown early — last week Gen. Ray Odierno, the American commander in Iraq, said that the number of troops had dropped to 49,700, roughly the number that would stay through next summer.

That is less than a third of the number of troops in Iraq during the surge in 2007. Under an agreement between Iraq and the United States, the remaining troops are to leave by the end of 2011, though some Iraqi and American officials say they think that the agreement may be renegotiated to allow for a longer American military presence.

The remaining "advise and assist" brigades will officially concentrate on supporting and training Iraqi security forces, protecting American personnel and facilities, and mounting counterterrorism operations.

Still, as Mr. Obama himself acknowledged Tuesday, the milestone came with all of the ambiguity and messiness that accompanied the war itself.

A political impasse, in place since March elections, has left Iraq without a permanent government just as the government in Baghdad was supposed to be asserting more control.

Republican critics of the president were quick to point out Tuesday that Mr. Obama opposed the troop surge that they credit for decreased violence in Iraq.

"Some leaders who opposed, criticized, and fought tooth-and-nail to stop the surge strategy now proudly claim credit for the results," Representative John A. Boehner of Ohio, the House Republican leader, told veterans at the national convention of the American Legion in Milwaukee.

CARL HULSE AND MARK MAZZETTI CONTRIBUTED REPORTING.

Fifteen Years Ago, America Destroyed My Country

OPINION | BY SINAN ANTOON | MARCH 19, 2018

WHEN I WAS 12, Saddam Hussein, vice president of Iraq at the time, carried out a huge purge and officially usurped total power. I was living in Baghdad then, and I developed an intuitive, visceral hatred of the dictator early on. That feeling only intensified and matured as I did. In the late 1990s, I wrote my first novel, "I'jaam: An Iraqi Rhapsody," about daily life under Saddam's authoritarian regime. Furat, the narrator, was a young college student studying English literature at Baghdad University, as I had. He ends up in prison for cracking a joke about the dictator. Furat hallucinates and imagines Saddam's fall, just as I often did. I hoped I would witness that moment, whether in Iraq or from afar.

I left Iraq a few months after the 1991 Gulf War and went to graduate school in the United States, where I've been ever since. In 2002, when the cheerleading for the Iraq war started, I was vehemently against the proposed invasion. The United States had consistently supported dictators in the Arab world and was not in the business of exporting democracy, irrespective of the Bush administration's slogans. I recalled sitting in my family's living room with my aunt when I was a teenager, watching Iraqi television and seeing Donald Rumsfeld visiting Baghdad as an emissary from Ronald Reagan and shaking hands with Saddam. That memory made Mr. Rumsfeld's words in 2002 about freedom and democracy for Iraqis seem hollow. Moreover, having lived through two previous wars (the Iran-Iraq war of 1980 to 1988 and the Gulf War of 1991), I knew that the actual objectives of war were always camouflaged by well-designed lies that exploit collective fear and perpetuate national myths.

I was one of about 500 Iraqis in the diaspora — of various ethnic and political backgrounds, many of whom were dissidents and victims of Saddam's regime — who signed a petition: "No to war on Iraq.

No to dictatorship." While condemning Saddam's reign of terror, we were against a "war that would cause more death and suffering" for innocent Iraqis and one that threatened to push the entire region into violent chaos. Our voices were not welcomed in mainstream media in the United States, which preferred the pro-war Iraqi-American who promised cheering crowds that would welcome invaders with "sweets and flowers." There were none.

The petition didn't make much of an impact. Fifteen years ago today, the invasion of Iraq began.

Three months later, I returned to Iraq for the first time since 1991 as part of a collective to film a documentary about Iraqis in a post-Saddam Iraq. We wanted to show my countrymen as three-dimensional beings, beyond the binary of Saddam versus the United States. In American media, Iraqis had been reduced to either victims of Saddam who longed for occupation or supporters and defenders of dictatorship who opposed the war. We wanted Iraqis to speak for themselves. For two weeks, we drove around Baghdad and spoke to many of its residents. Some were still hopeful, despite being drained by years of sanctions and dictatorship. But many were furious and worried about what was to come. The signs were already there: the typical arrogance and violence of a colonial occupying power.

My short visit only confirmed my conviction and fear that the invasion would spell disaster for Iraqis. Removing Saddam was just a byproduct of another objective: dismantling the Iraqi state and its institutions. That state was replaced with a dysfunctional and corrupt semi-state. We were still filming in Baghdad when L. Paul Bremer III, the head of the Coalition Provisional Authority, announced the formation of the so-called Governing Council in July 2003. The names of its members were each followed by their sect and ethnicity. Many of the Iraqis we spoke to on that day were upset with institutionalization of an ethno-sectarian quota system. Ethnic and sectarian tensions already existed, but their translation into political currency was toxic. Those unsavory characters on the governing council, most of whom were allies of the United States from the preceding decade, went on to loot the country, making it one of the most corrupt in the world.

We were fortunate to have been able to shoot our film in that brief period during which there was relative public security. Shortly after our visit, Iraq descended into violence; suicide bombings became the norm. The invasion made my country a magnet for terrorists ("We'll fight them there so we don't have to fight them here," President George W. Bush had said), and Iraq later descended into a sectarian civil war that claimed the lives of hundreds of thousands of civilians and displaced hundreds of thousands more, irrevocably changing the country's demography.

The next time I returned to Baghdad was in 2013. The American tanks were gone, but the effects of the occupation were everywhere. I had low expectations, but I was still disheartened by the ugliness of the city where I had grown up and horrified by how dysfunctional, difficult and dangerous daily life had become for the great majority of Iraqis.

My last visit was in April 2017. I flew from New York, where I now live, to Kuwait, where I was giving a lecture. An Iraqi friend and I crossed the border by land. I was going to the city of Basra, in the south of Iraq. Basra was the only major Iraqi city I had not visited before. I was going to sign my books at the Friday book market of al-Farahidi Street, a weekly gathering for bibliophiles modeled after the famous Mutanabbi Street book market in Baghdad. I was driven around by friends. I didn't expect the beautiful Basra I'd seen on 1970s postcards. That city had long disappeared. But the Basra I saw was so exhausted and polluted. The city had suffered a great deal during the Iran-Iraq war, and its decline accelerated after 2003. Basra was pale, dilapidated and chaotic thanks to the rampant corruption. Its rivers are polluted and ebbing. Nonetheless, I made a pilgrimage to the famous statue of Iraq's greatest poet, Badr Shakir al-Sayyab.

One of the few sources of joy for me during these short visits were the encounters with Iraqis who had read my novels and were moved by them. These were novels I had written from afar, and through them, I tried to grapple with the painful disintegration of an entire country and the destruction of its social fabric. These texts are haunted by the ghosts of the dead, just as their author is.

No one knows for certain how many Iraqis have died as a result of the invasion 15 years ago. Some credible estimates put the number at more than one million. You can read that sentence again. The invasion of Iraq is often spoken of in the United States as a "blunder," or even a "colossal mistake." It was a crime. Those who perpetrated it are still at large. Some of them have even been rehabilitated thanks to the horrors of Trumpism and a mostly amnesiac citizenry. (A year ago, I watched Mr. Bush on "The Ellen DeGeneres Show," dancing and talking about his paintings.) The pundits and "experts" who sold us the war still go on doing what they do. I never thought that Iraq could ever be worse than it was during Saddam's reign, but that is what America's war achieved and bequeathed to Iraqis.

SINAN ANTOON (@SINANANTOON) IS THE AUTHOR, MOST RECENTLY, OF THE NOVEL "THE BAGHDAD EUCHARIST."

15 Years Ago, I Helped Start a War That Hasn't Ended

BY MATT UFFORD | MARCH 20, 2018

WHEN I DEPLOYED to Iraq in 2003, there was no war. We had to start it.

As a lieutenant in charge of six tanks (four active-duty crews, two reserve), I gave a preinvasion talk to my platoon before rolling out. It was 15 years ago, and I was 24 — older than all but two of the 23 crewmen. It was a moment I had long fantasized about, inspired by the fist-pumping motivational speeches that rouse the troops in war movies like "Gladiator" and "Patton."

Behind a line of tanks, on a stretch of Kuwaiti sand as flat and featureless as my courage, I adopted a folksy tone. "I know y'all were probably looking forward to a big 'Braveheart' talk, but you know me — I'm not one to speechify." I paused, tried to stop my voice from shaking and failed. "I'm just like the rest of you: I've never been to combat, so I don't know what it's like. But I want to tell you all that it's O.K. to be scared." I'm not sure whom I was trying to convince more: my Marines or myself. "What's not O.K. is to let that fear overcome you. No panicking. We're all well trained, and as long as we go with our training and make quick decisions, we're gonna accomplish the mission and be fine. Tank commanders, you know what I expect." That was it. No one responded with a battle cry.

Of the 80 or so Marines in Delta Company, First Tank Battalion, only one of us had ever seen combat: a gunnery sergeant who fought in Desert Storm. His face was creased and leathery from a decade in the Mojave outpost of Twentynine Palms, and he had the unhurried gait of a man whose cartilage was shot from a career of clambering on and off no-skid steel. Soon many of us would look more like him than our selves.

We spent the weeks before the invasion in Kuwait waiting for orders, fighting off boredom. We adjusted the sights of our tanks, banged on the tracks with heavy tools, went over the assault plan, pored through satellite imagery, cleaned our weapons, practiced speed drills with gas masks and still had more empty hours than busy ones. We joked that we wanted the war to start just for a break from the monotony.

We filled the time with card games, pranks, rumors and — occasionally, quietly — our thoughts and fears about combat. My friend Travis Carlson had a specific fear of being shot through the neck. I couldn't decide if I was more afraid of death or of the general unknown of what waited for us once we crossed the border. Nothing loomed larger, though, than the desire to live up to the storied history of the Marine Corps. I didn't need to stand shoulder to shoulder with the legend of Chesty Puller and his five Navy Crosses or the corps' long list of Medal of Honor recipients, but I couldn't let them down either.

The case for the invasion was thin — or rather, it was thick, but, we now know, filled with faulty intelligence, half-truths and a fervor for war that was unsated by the conflict in Afghanistan. Back in the United States, President George W. Bush told the nation on March 19 that it was time to free the people of Iraq and "defend the world from grave danger." Within hours, thousands of troops, including my battalion, crossed the border to look for Saddam Hussein's weapons of mass destruction.

Our company commander stressed that we should exact only as much harm as the mission required, but a tank is not a scalpel. When we drove across a field, newly planted crops flew skyward behind our vehicles in great roostertails of earth. When we provided supporting fire to an engineer detonating mines, we felled trees with our machine guns. Inside the tank, we hardly felt a bump when we crushed cars under our treads. We brought war everywhere we went.

The pace was relentless: a race to an objective, a brief engagement — tanks have a way of ending battles quickly — and then back on the highway. We drove all day and all night, from Basra to Nasiriyah to Diwaniyah, stopping only to refuel. Over the course of a week, I slept 10 hours. No one up the chain of command seemed to care about sleep until one of Charlie Company's tanks drove off a bridge over the Euphrates in the middle of the night. It settled in the riverbed upside-down, and the four Marines inside died.

We doglegged east to Numaniyah, then continued to push northwest on Highway 6. That's where my friend Brian McPhillips of Second Tank Battalion was fatally shot in the head, but I wouldn't hear the news for another two weeks. Information rarely travels laterally in war. I was a few miles from the ambush that killed him when I learned that my platoon would lead the battalion over the Diyala River and into Baghdad.

The bridge was partly destroyed. Two-thirds of the way to the far side, a chunk of the span was gone, leaving pieces of exposed rebar and a clear view to the water below. Combat engineers laid a make-shift bridge over the gap. I asked the engineer lieutenant if it would hold a tank's weight. "I think so," he said.

As the platoon commander, I could dictate which tank went over first, but it wasn't really a choice. It had barely been a week since Charlie Company's Marines drowned in the Euphrates; I left the hatch of my cupola all the way open, prepared to jump free of the vehicle if it went in the water.

As we came over the crest of the bridge, a man on the far side of the river fired an AK-47 at us. This was inconvenient. I was trying to guide our driver onto the engineer's bridge while scanning the landscape for other threats; being shot at felt gratuitous.

"Co-ax, fire," I said.

"On the way," my gunner replied, and ended someone's life with the tank's 7.62-millimeter coaxial machine gun.

As he fired, I caught sight of a Soviet-made T-72 tank dug into a defensive position. I grabbed the override to rotate the turret while giving a hasty fire command to my gunner. The thunderous boom echoed across the battlefield, and I saw the orange spark of steel on steel. Secondary explosions followed as the T-72's ammunition cooked off. On the radio, I reported the kills and called off the artillery mission, which was well inside the "danger close" range of 600 meters. I could feel the overpressure from the bursting shells, a concussive force that shook my cheeks.

"Hey, sir?" It was my driver. "Are those mines?"

We had driven across the bridge into a minefield. It ended up being a long day.

Baghdad fell on April 9. After the resistance on the outskirts of the city, we expected a devastating battle on urban terrain. Instead, we rolled into the capital and were greeted by cheers. It felt as if my chest might burst from relief and pride: The job was done, and all my men were alive. I had been a part of the longest inland assault in Marine Corps history.

Ten days later, First Tank Battalion left the capital; our vehicles were "too aggressive" of a posture for the peacekeeping mission to come. The occupation needed military police officers and translators; we had 70-ton vehicles with high-explosive anti-tank rounds. It seemed like a rash decision — and indeed, tanks would be a mainstay of the Marine mission in Iraq for years to come — but that didn't stop us from whooping with excitement as we left the city. The occupation was someone else's problem now.

Fifteen years later, the invasion is a footnote to the war, and the aftermath is filled with too much death and dishonor for me to ever regret leaving the service without another deployment. But there was a moment — before Abu Ghraib, before Falluja, before the Haditha massacre, or the Surge, or the drawdown, or ISIS — that I still cherish. On the day we rolled into Baghdad as victors, First Tank Battalion encamped in the shadow of the giant turquoise dome of the Al-Shaheed Monument, enjoying the protection of the man-made lakes around it. We were abuzz with the joy of being alive and having accomplished our mission. I shared a kettle of coffee with one of my sergeants, and I told him I wanted to come back to Baghdad one day to see what it might look like in peace and prosperity. As the sun set on a liberated city, golden light turned the dusty sidewalks to warm coral, and for a moment it felt as if the war were over.

CHAPTER 5

The War on Terror

Following the attack on the World Trade Center, the United
States declared a war on terror and invaded Afghanistan, leading to one of the most protracted military engagements in the
nation's history. Over the years, the nature of the conflict has
changed, resulting in a murky set of goals. President Barack
Obama announced a plan for withdrawal at the same time as
he stepped up the use of drone warfare in Afghanistan as well
as in Pakistan and Yemen. As of 2018, the U.S. continues to
have troops in the region with no plans to withdraw.

U.S. and Britain Strike Afghanistan, Aiming at Bases and Terrorist Camps; Bush Warns 'Taliban Will Pay a Price'

BY PATRICK E. TYLER | OCT. 8, 2001

STRIKING AT NIGHT from aircraft carriers and distant bases, the United
States and Britain launched a powerful barrage of cruise missiles and
long-range bombers against Afghanistan today to try to destroy the
terrorist training camps of Osama bin Laden's Qaeda network and the
Taliban government that has protected it.

"On my orders, the United States military has begun strikes,"
President Bush said in a televised statement from the White House
at 1 p.m., just more than half an hour after the first explosions were
reported in Kabul, the Afghan capital.

"These carefully targeted actions are designed to disrupt the use of
Afghanistan as a terrorist base of operations and to attack the military

capability of the Taliban regime," Mr. Bush said.

The Taliban was warned, he said, to meet America's demands to surrender Mr. bin Laden, stop supporting terrorism and release foreign aid workers they hold. "None of these demands were met," he said. "And now, the Taliban will pay a price."

"Today we focus on Afghanistan," he added, but "the battle is broader." Alluding to the Sept. 11 terror attacks that destroyed the World Trade Center, damaged the Pentagon and killed more than 5,000 people, Mr. Bush again warned that nations that sponsor or protect "outlaws and killers of innocents" will "take that lonely path at their own peril."

The skies over Kabul lit up with flashes, and thunderous explosions rumbled through the night, witnesses said. The Taliban fired antiaircraft guns into the dark sky, and their tracers could be seen by residents of the capital and around the cities of Kandahar and Jalalabad, strongholds of the radical Islamic regime.

Mr. Bush's statement was followed by one from Prime Minister Tony Blair of Britain. Both leaders emphasized that the military campaign was not "a war with Islam," as Mr. Blair asserted, though no Muslim country took part directly in the attacks and many refused to allow offensive operations to be staged from their territory.

Mr. Bush said "we are the friends of almost a billion" people worldwide "who practice the Islamic faith."

Defense Secretary Donald H. Rumsfeld noted that the United States had sent its armed forces five times in the last decade to defend oppressed Muslim populations — in Kuwait, northern Iraq, Somalia, Bosnia and Kosovo.

Shortly after Mr. Bush spoke, Mr. bin Laden issued his own threat. On what appeared to be a recorded videotape beamed worldwide by CNN, he staked a claim to lead all Muslims in the fight against America, casting it as the murderer of Iraqis and of Palestinians oppressed by Israel, America's friend.

Mr. bin Laden blessed the hijackers who staged the Sept. 11 attacks and warned, "I swear to God that America will not live in peace before peace reigns in Palestine, and before all the army of infidels depart the land of Muhammad."

Abdul Salam Zaeef, the Taliban's ambassador to Pakistan, called the assault a terrorist attack and vowed that America would "never achieve its goal."

The opening aerial campaign could go on for a week and will be followed by ground operations by Special Forces units to garner information and hunt down the leaders of the Qaeda network, administration officials indicated.

Gen. Richard B. Myers, the new chairman of the Joint Chiefs of Staff, said the bombardment began at 12:30 p.m., Eastern time, and included 15 land-based bombers and 25 strike aircraft from aircraft carriers. Their weapons included precision-guided bombs, and American warships and British submarines fired 50 Tomahawk cruise missiles.

A B-52 pilot who took part in today's attack said by telephone afterward that the nose of one of the bombers had been repainted shortly before the mission to read, "NYPD, We Remember."

Mr. Rumsfeld said Mr. bin Laden was not a specific target. The initial bombing, he said, was intended "to create conditions for sustained antiterrorist" operations against his organization.

Mr. Bush did not mention Mr. bin Laden in his remarks, suggesting that the White House was seeking to lower expectations of his capture even as Central Intelligence Agency and Special Forces teams were said to be working feverishly to locate him. He is suspected of being the mastermind behind terrorist strikes on Americans and American interests even before the Sept. 11 assault — in Somalia in 1993, on two embassies in East Africa in 1998 and on the destroyer Cole in Yemen a year ago.

A spokesman for Al Jazeera television, in the Persian Gulf emirate of Qatar, said Mr. bin Laden's words had arrived at the network's satellite uplink station in Kabul.

"People bring tapes," said Omar Bec, head of news gathering for Al Jazeera. "They deliver them to the office or leave them at the door." This tape, he said, "was delivered today to us."

"We, honest to God, don't know when it was shot, where it was shot, or how it was shot," Mr. Bec said.

Mr. Bush ordered the attack 26 days after hijackers, several of them now linked by investigators to Mr. bin Laden's network, seized four airliners, crashing two of them into the World Trade Center in New York and one into the Pentagon in Washington. A fourth crashed into a Pennsylvania field after passengers apparently tried to over-power the hijackers.

Mr. Rumsfeld made clear that the United States was seeking to orchestrate the overthrow of the Taliban by providing military aid and "developing relationships with groups in Afghanistan that oppose the Taliban regime" and the "terrorists they support." The major opposition force is the Northern Alliance, but he also said disaffected members of the Taliban and other groups could coalesce to challenge the Taliban.

The secretary said the goals of the military operation were to punish the Taliban for "harboring terrorists," to "acquire intelligence" that will help future operations against Al Qaeda and to weaken the Taliban so severely that they will not be able to withstand an opposition assault.

Another goal, Mr. Rumsfeld said, is to provide relief aid "to Afghans suffering truly oppressive living conditions under the Taliban regime."

To that end, the Pentagon today sent two C-17 cargo planes flying from Germany to drop 37,500 packets of food and medical supplies to help perhaps hundreds of thousands of refugees who may flee Afghan cities during the bombing campaign.

With no Muslim government taking part in the attack — in contrast to the case a decade ago when Arab forces helped to eject Iraq's Army from Kuwait — Mr. Bush nonetheless stated that "we are supported by the collective will of the world."

"More than 40 countries in the Middle East, Africa, Europe and across Asia have granted air transit and landing rights," he said.

The Federal Bureau of Investigation, concerned about more ter-rorist attacks, urged law enforcement agencies across the country to move to their highest level of alert.

"All law enforcement agencies have been asked to evaluate whether additional local security measures are warranted in light of the military operations and the current threat level," the F.B.I. said.

Security at public buildings and key installations was reported high across the United States and at American missions abroad as administration officials — and the public — braced for any attempted counterstrikes by terrorists.

Vice President Dick Cheney was placed in a secure location, while Mr. Bush remained at the White House. The American Embassy in Riyadh, Saudi Arabia, closed until further notice. The State Department urged Americans overseas "to exercise caution."

The United States warned its citizens in Indonesia to prepare for evacuation after the radical Islamic Defenders Front warned that it would begin attacking Americans and other foreigners if Indonesia did not break diplomatic relations with Washington within 72 hours.

Secretary of State Colin L. Powell was scheduled to visit India and Pakistan at week's end, "to keep things balanced between them," an administration official said.

Though the opening hours of the campaign were dominated by images of fuzzy explosions beamed out of Afghanistan by television networks, intensive diplomacy was under way behind the scenes to hold together the coalition.

One concern was that Iran had called a meeting of the 56-member Organization of Islamic Conference, which will meet in Qatar on Wednesday. An Iranian official today called the American and British assault "unacceptable," but stopped short of saying Iran condemned it.

"It was conditionally condemned," said Hamid Reza Asefi, a Foreign Ministry spokesman, because of its potential "to result in the loss of life among civilians."

Still, the prospect that the Islamic Conference, which represents a billion Muslims worldwide, might declare opposition to the assault loomed as a crucial test for the Bush administration's ability to sustain support for military action. Even Palestinian leaders said they were hoping for a "joint" Muslim position on the American strikes.

Israel today offered political support, including the all-important step of refraining from direct military operations that might undermine Muslim support for the fight against terrorism. In doing so, Israel repeated the step it took during the Persian Gulf war in 1991.

A statement issued by the office of Prime Minister Ariel Sharon said that in the last three days Secretary Powell had kept the Israeli leader "informed of the preparations for the U.S. attack." It added that "Israel helps and will provide its help but is not taking part in the war."

Today's attacks set off anti-American protests in Pakistan, where some of the country's most influential Islamic clerics called on Muslims "to support their Afghan brothers" against American "aggression." Gen. Pervez Musharraf, Pakistan's president, placed a militant cleric under house arrest and re-organized his military command to limit dissent among top generals.

At the White House, Mr. Bush telephoned leaders around the globe. He spoke with President Vladimir V. Putin of Russia just before the attack began. Mr. Bush and Secretary Powell also spoke with leaders of Canada, Australia, Germany and France, which have "pledged forces" for the operation, the president said.

President Jacques Chirac of France told his countrymen today that "our forces will take part" in coming operations "in a spirit of solidarity and responsibility."

"At this stage," he added, "French ships are associated with this operation."

In Berlin, Chancellor Gerhard Schröder said Germany would join with France "to make its contribution." In Ottawa, Prime Minister Jean Chrétien said Canada would provide "a number of units" for unspecified operations to come. China offered a cautious endorsement.

In Iraq, President Saddam Hussein called an emergency meeting of his inner cabinet, and a communiqué issued afterward said,

"True believers cannot but condemn this act, not because it has been committed by America against a Muslim people but because it is an aggression perpetrated outside international law."

Long War Is Seen

BY STEVEN LEE MYERS WITH ALAN COWELL | OCT. 12, 2001

THE UNITED STATES and Britain made clear today that they are marshaling for a long engagement in Afghanistan, stretching into next summer and including the possible use of ground forces.

Adm. Sir Michael Boyce, the chief of the British defense staff, said the allies "must expect to go through the winter and into next summer at the very least."

President Bush said tonight that the military operation would continue for days, months or even years .

Admiral Boyce, Britain's top commander, said that if ground forces are called for, a commando brigade of the Royal Marines now taking part in exercises in Oman would most likely be used.

"They are our expert mountain and winter warfare troops," he said. "If we were to be thinking about doing any operations in Afghanistan on the ground, then clearly they would be one of the units we would give very close consideration to."

At the Pentagon, Defense Secretary Donald H. Rumsfeld was circumspect today when asked if the United States might use a significant number of ground troops inside Afghanistan. But he made clear that preparations were in progress for using such troops.

The overall strategy American and British officials are sketching is one of destroying Afghanistan's command and control structure from the air, thereby clearing the way for military operations by speciality units and for covert operations already under way.

The option of pursuing other terrorist groups in other Arab countries is still to be explored. But American officials said they are concerned that allies such as Egypt and Saudi Arabia do not yet fully grasp that Mr. Bush's "new war" against terrorism may not end with the elimination of Osama bin Laden and could involve chasing terrorist groups in other countries.

Mr. Bush said tonight that the administration is also hoping that Arab allies will help choke off the terrorists' money supply and take other legal steps.

"You have to prepare for the worst and hope for the best," he said. "But we expect it to be a long effort. And we're getting arranged so that we can sustain ourselves over a period of time."

The United States already has sent troops from the 10th Mountain Division from Fort Drum, N.Y., to Uzbekistan, and other forces have begun to arrive in Pakistan.

Military officials said that the Pentagon has recently issued new deployment orders to unspecified units.

Heavy bombing of Taliban military forces and installations continued around the clock, with American bombers and fighters using cluster bombs to attack troop concentrations and other, huge bombs to destroy underground fortifications. Many of the targets were near Kabul and Kandahar, a stronghold of the Taliban government.

Underground command posts used by the Taliban government's forces, as well as those used by Al Qaeda, the terrorist network of Osama bin Laden, were being attacked with enormous, 5,000-pound bombs known as "bunker busters," as well as by special bombs designed to penetrate deep into the earth before exploding in hideouts excavated in the rugged Afghan mountains. One of the underground bunkers was south of Jalalabad, officials said.

"I have seen several examples where there were enormous secondary explosions, in some cases that went on for several hours after targeting underground facilities," Mr. Rumsfeld said. That could be an indication that ammunition or fuel was stored there.

Britain, America's closest ally and the nation most actively participating in the United States-led military operation against Mr. bin Laden and the Taliban regime that supports him, has often spoken more pointedly than Washington about their joint effort. The British high command has helped draft the campaign plan, according to British officials.

The British, who will be carrying out special operations along with the Americans, believe that the attacks will take time. A senior British official said the aim of the military campaign was to "keep shaking it up until the pieces you want come out," meaning that the campaign would keep Mr. bin Laden and his followers off balance "until you start to catch people."

The official said one option was to establish an allied bridgehead inside Afghanistan as a base from which to pursue commando and special forces forays to seek Mr. bin Laden. But the official said that both Britain and the United States wanted that base to be independent from the Northern Alliance, the Afghanistan force that has been fighting the Taliban and that is regarded with suspicion by Pakistan.

A prolonged operation would have far-reaching political implications abroad as well as in the United States. Pakistan, for example, wants a quick war and the speedy exit of American troops from the region. That would help Pakistan cope with the problem of instability.

But the signs today indicated a long campaign, not a short one. Almost all of the Air Force's fleet of more than 100 heavy transport aircraft were being used to rush equipment and supplies to the region, the military said.

The aircraft carrier Kitty Hawk has arrived in the Arabian sea, where it is to serve as a platform for troops and helicopters. A large force of marines is at sea there, too.

At a memorial service at the Pentagon today for those killed in the Sept. 11 attack, President Bush said America would "never relent" in the campaign against terrorism.

"In the missions ahead for the military, you will have everything you need, every resource, every weapon, every means to assure full victory for the United States and the cause of freedom," he said.

"There will be times of swift, dramatic action," he continued. "There will be times of steady, quiet progress. Over time, with patience and precision, the terrorists will be pursued. They will be isolated, surrounded, cornered, until there is no place to run or hide or rest."

After the ceremony, Mr. Rumsfeld said for the first time that the United States was communicating with factions opposed to the Taliban government and using the information to develop targets for attack inside the country, although he and other officials said the exchange stopped short of telling Northern Alliance fighters what Taliban forces would be struck.

Northern Alliance officials have said that American and British special forces are working in territory controlled by them, and that the forces are gathering intelligence for the allies.

Without acknowledging that, Mr. Rumsfeld said that "the United States is in communication with people on the ground in terms of gathering information as to military targets." He said the information comes from "a variety of places."

Maj. Gen. Henry P. Osman, director of operations for the Joint Chiefs of Staff, said at a Pentagon briefing today that targets hit Wednesday included "troop training facilities, military forces, motor pools, and missile and radar sites." Bombers flying from Diego Garcia, jets from two aircraft carriers, and three Tomahawk missiles from an American submarine were used, he said.

Officials said similar targets were being hit tonight.

The Bush administration has not spoken of a specific timetable for the military action in Afghanistan. President Bush has suggested that the United States would be involved in a long struggle, but never suggested that the military operation could take so long.

British officials have been telling reporters for days that the military operation may be drawn out for a variety of military and political reasons. One reason is the sense that the airstrikes may not be decisive. But there are other factors, including the winter weather, which could interfere with ground operations, and the beginning of the Muslim holy month of Ramadan on Nov. 15.

A Merciful War

OPINION | BY NICHOLAS D. KRISTOF | FEB. 1, 2002

ONE OF THE UNCOMFORTABLE realities of the war on terrorism is that we Americans have killed many more people in Afghanistan than died in the attack on the World Trade Center.

Over the last couple of months I've tried to tabulate the Afghan death toll. My best guess is that we killed 8,000 to 12,000 Taliban fighters, along with about 1,000 Afghan civilians.

So what is the lesson of this? Is it that while pretending to take the high road, we have actually slaughtered more people than Osama bin Laden has? Or that military responses are unjustifiable because huge numbers of innocents inevitably are killed?

No, it's just the opposite.

Our experience there demonstrates that troops can advance humanitarian goals just as much as doctors or aid workers can. By my calculations, our invasion of Afghanistan may end up saving one million lives over the next decade.

Ever since Vietnam, the West has been deeply squeamish about the use of force — particularly European and American liberals, who are often so horrified by bloodshed involving innocents that they believe nothing can justify it. But Afghanistan shows that guns and bombs can save lives as much as scalpels and IV tubes do.

Look at the numbers. In each of the last few years, without anyone paying much attention, 225,000 children died in Afghanistan before the age of 5, along with 15,000 women who died during pregnancy or childbirth. There was no way to save those lives under the Taliban; indeed, international organizations were retreating from Afghanistan even before 9/11 because of the arrests of Christian aid workers.

But now aid is pouring in and lives are being saved on an enormous scale. Unicef, for example, has vaccinated 734,000 children against measles over the last two months, in a country where virtually no one had been vaccinated against the disease in the previous 10 years. Because measles often led to death in Afghanistan, the vaccination campaign will save at least 35,000 children's lives each year.

"You're going to see an immediate jump" in Afghanistan's health statistics and school attendance, says Mark Malloch Brown, the head of the United Nations Development Program. But he adds that truly building the country up will be a hard slog over 10 or 20 years.

Of course, the gains depend on stability in Afghanistan, and that is not guaranteed. But if the West lives up to its obligations to help Afghanistan, and not abandon it as we all did a decade ago, then the potential savings in human lives are staggering.

Heidi J. Larson of Unicef says that if all goes well, child and maternal mortality rates will drop in half in Afghanistan over the next five years. That would mean 112,000 fewer children and 7,500 fewer pregnant women dying each year.

Likewise, a desperate rush to train 20,000 new teachers and open new schools means that some 1.5 million Afghan children will be able to enroll in elementary school when the term begins next month — more than double the number of children who were in school a year ago.

Denunciations of the American bombing in Afghanistan pop up regularly in the United States and even more boldly in Europe and the Muslim world. A Pakistani columnist, Humayun Gauhar, described the war in his country's typically subdued prose: "The stench of Afghan flesh, the sweet smell of their children's blood (garnished lightly with one dead American) has overpowered the quest for prime target Osama bin Laden."

Yet these critics seemed less exercised by the much larger number of preventable deaths in Afghanistan from routine ailments. I've sat in mud huts with parents sobbing as their children died of diarrhea, and trust me: Their grief is every bit as crushing as that of parents who lose children to bombs.

Working from United Nations figures, if Afghanistan eventually improves just to the wretched levels of neighboring Pakistan, that would mean 115,000 fewer deaths a year of children under the age of 5, along with 9,600 fewer women dying in pregnancy each year.

All this underscores a simple truth, and enough time has passed since Vietnam that we should be able to acknowledge it: Military intervention, even if it means lost innocent lives on both sides, can serve the most humanitarian of goals.

How a 'Good War' in Afghanistan Went Bad

BY DAVID ROHDE AND DAVID E. SANGER | AUG. 12, 2007

TWO YEARS AFTER the Taliban fell to an American-led coalition, a group of NATO ambassadors landed in Kabul, Afghanistan, to survey what appeared to be a triumph — a fresh start for a country ripped apart by years of war with the Soviets and brutal repression by religious extremists.

With a senior American diplomat, R. Nicholas Burns, leading the way, they thundered around the country in Black Hawk helicopters, with little fear for their safety. They strolled quiet streets in Kandahar and sipped tea with tribal leaders. At a briefing from the United States Central Command, they were told that the Taliban were now a "spent force."

"Some of us were saying, 'Not so fast,' " Mr. Burns, now the under secretary of state for political affairs, recalled. "While not a strategic threat, a number of us assumed that the Taliban was too enmeshed in Afghan society to just disappear."

But that skepticism had never taken hold in Washington. Since the 2001 war, American intelligence agencies had reported that the Taliban were so decimated they no longer posed a threat, according to two senior intelligence officials who reviewed the reports.

The American sense of victory had been so robust that the top C.I.A. specialists and elite Special Forces units who had helped liberate Afghanistan had long since moved on to the next war, in Iraq.

Those sweeping miscalculations were part of a pattern of assessments and decisions that helped send what many in the American military call "the good war" off course.

Like Osama bin Laden and his deputies, the Taliban had found refuge in Pakistan and regrouped as the American focus wavered. Taliban fighters seeped back over the border, driving up the suicide attacks and roadside bombings by as much as 25 percent this spring, and forcing NATO and American troops into battles to retake previously liberated villages in southern Afghanistan.

They have scored some successes recently, and since the 2001 invasion, there have been improvements in health care, education and the economy, as well as the quality of life in the cities. But Afghanistan's embattled president, Hamid Karzai, said in Washington last week that security in his country had "definitely deteriorated." One former national security official called that "a very diplomatic understatement."

President Bush's critics have long contended that the Iraq war has diminished America's effort in Afghanistan, which the administration has denied, but an examination of how the policy unfolded within the administration reveals a deep divide over how to proceed in Afghanistan and a series of decisions that at times seemed to relegate it to an afterthought as Iraq unraveled.

Statements from the White House, including from the president, in support of Afghanistan were resolute, but behind them was a halting, sometimes reluctant commitment to solving Afghanistan's myriad problems, according to dozens of interviews in the United States, at NATO headquarters in Brussels and in Kabul, the Afghan capital.

At critical moments in the fight for Afghanistan, the Bush administration diverted scarce intelligence and reconstruction resources to Iraq, including elite C.I.A. teams and Special Forces units involved in the search for terrorists. As sophisticated Predator spy planes rolled off assembly lines in the United States, they were shipped to Iraq, undercutting the search for Taliban and terrorist leaders, according to senior military and intelligence officials.

As defense secretary, Donald H. Rumsfeld claimed credit for toppling the Taliban with light, fast forces. But in a move that foreshadowed America's trouble in Iraq, he failed to anticipate the need for more forces after the old government was gone, and blocked an early proposal from Colin L. Powell, then the secretary of state, and Mr. Karzai, the administration's handpicked president, for a large inter-

American soldiers during an operation in Zabul Province in 2006.

national force. As the situation deteriorated, Mr. Rumsfeld and other administration officials reversed course and cajoled European allies into sending troops.

When it came to reconstruction, big goals were announced, big projects identified. Yet in the year Mr. Bush promised a "Marshall Plan" for Afghanistan, the country received less assistance per capita than did postconflict Bosnia and Kosovo, or even desperately poor Haiti, according to a RAND Corporation study. Washington has spent an average of $3.4 billion a year reconstructing Afghanistan, less than half of what it has spent in Iraq, according to the Congressional Research Service.

The White House contends that the troop level in Afghanistan was increased when needed and that it now stands at 23,500. But a senior American commander said that even as the military force grew last year, he was surprised to discover that "I could count on the fingers of one or two hands the number of U.S. government agricultural experts" in Afghanistan, where 80 percent of the economy is agricultural. A $300 million project authorized by Congress for small businesses was never financed.

Underlying many of the decisions, officials say, was a misapprehension about what Americans would find on the ground in Afghanistan. "The perception was that Afghans hated foreigners and that the Iraqis would welcome us," said James Dobbins, the administration's former special envoy for Afghanistan. "The reverse turned out to be the case."

Secretary of State Condoleezza Rice defended the administration's policy, saying, "I don't buy the argument that Afghanistan was starved of resources." Yet she said: "I don't think the U.S. government had what it needed for reconstructing a country. We did it ad hoc in the Balkans, and then in Afghanistan, and then in Iraq."

In interviews, three former American ambassadors to Afghanistan were more critical of Washington's record.

"I said from the get-go that we didn't have enough money and we didn't have enough soldiers," said Robert P. Finn, who was the ambassador in 2002 and 2003. "I'm saying the same thing six years later."

Zalmay Khalilzad, who was the next ambassador and is now the American ambassador to the United Nations, said, "I do think that state-building and nation-building, we came to that reluctantly," adding that "I think more could have been done earlier on these issues."

And Ronald E. Neumann, who replaced Mr. Khalilzad in Kabul, said, "The idea that we could just hunt terrorists and we didn't have to do nation-building, and we could just leave it alone, that was a large mistake."

A BIG PROMISE, UNFULFILLED

After months of arguing unsuccessfully for a far larger effort in Afghanistan, Mr. Dobbins received an unexpected call in April 2002. Mr. Bush, he was told, was planning to proclaim America's commitment to rebuild Afghanistan.

"I got a call from the White House speech writers saying they were writing a speech and did I see any reason not to cite the Marshall

Plan," Mr. Dobbins recalled, referring to the American rebuilding of postwar Europe. "I said, 'No, I saw no objections', so they put it in the speech."

On April 17, Mr. Bush traveled to the Virginia Military Institute, where Gen. George C. Marshall trained a century ago. "Marshall knew that our military victory against enemies in World War II had to be followed by a moral victory that resulted in better lives for individual human beings," Mr. Bush said, calling Marshall's work "a beacon to light the path that we, too, must follow."

Mr. Bush had belittled "nation building" while campaigning for president 18 months earlier. But aware that Afghans had felt abandoned before, including by his father's administration after the Soviets left in 1989, he vowed to avoid the syndrome of "initial success, followed by long years of floundering and ultimate failure.

"We're not going to repeat that mistake," he said. "We're tough, we're determined, we're relentless. We will stay until the mission is done."

The speech, which received faint notice in the United States, fueled expectations in Afghanistan and bolstered Mr. Karzai's stature before an Afghan grand council meeting in June 2002 at which Mr. Karzai was formally chosen to lead the government.

Yet privately, some senior officials, including Mr. Rumsfeld, were concerned that Afghanistan was a morass where the United States could achieve little, according to administration officials involved in the debate.

Within hours of the president's speech, Mr. Rumsfeld announced his own approach at a Pentagon news conference.

"The last thing you're going to hear from this podium is someone thinking they know how Afghanistan ought to organize itself," he said. "They're going to have to figure it out. They're going to have to grab ahold of that thing and do something. And we're there to help."

But the help was slow in coming. Despite Mr. Bush's promise in Virginia, in the months that followed his April speech, no detailed reconstruction plan emerged from the administration. Some senior administration officials lay the blame on the National Security Council, which is charged with making sure the president's foreign policy is carried out.

The stagnation reflected tension within the administration over how large a role the United States should play in stabilizing a country after toppling its government, former officials say.

After the fall of the Taliban in December 2001, Mr. Powell and Ms. Rice, then the national security adviser, argued in confidential sessions that if the United States now lost Afghanistan, America's image would be damaged, officials said. In a February 2002 meeting in the White House Situation Room, Mr. Powell proposed that American troops join the small international peacekeeping force patrolling Kabul and help Mr. Karzai extend his influence beyond the capital.

Mr. Powell said in an interview that his model was the 1989 invasion of Panama, where American troops spread out across the country after ousting the Noriega government. "The strategy has to be to take charge of the whole country by military force, police or other means," he said.

Richard N. Haass, a former director of policy planning at the State Department, said informal talks with European officials had led him to believe that a force of 20,000 to 40,000 peacekeepers could be recruited, half from Europe, half from the United States.

But Mr. Rumsfeld contended that European countries were unwilling to contribute more troops, said Douglas J. Feith, then the Pentagon's under secretary for policy. He said Mr. Rumsfeld felt that sending American troops would reduce pressure on Europeans to contribute, and could provoke Afghans' historic resistance to invaders and divert American forces from hunting terrorists. Mr. Rumsfeld declined to comment.

Some officials said they also feared confusion if European forces viewed the task as peacekeeping while the American military saw its job as fighting terrorists. Ms. Rice, despite having argued for fully backing the new Karzai government, took a middle position, leaving the issue unresolved. "I felt that we needed more forces, but there was a real problem, which you continue to see to this day, with the dual role," she said.

Ultimately, Mr. Powell's proposal died. "The president, the vice president, the secretary of defense, the national security staff, all of them were skeptical of an ambitious project in Afghanistan," Mr. Haass said. "I didn't see support."

Mr. Dobbins, the former special envoy, said Mr. Powell "seemed resigned."

"I said this wasn't going to be fully satisfactory," he recalled. "And he said, 'Well, it's the best we could do.' "

In the end, the United States deployed 8,000 troops to Afghanistan in 2002, with orders to hunt Taliban and Qaeda members, and not to engage in peacekeeping or reconstruction. The 4,000-member international peacekeeping force did not venture beyond Kabul.

As an alternative, officials hatched a loosely organized plan for Afghans to secure the country themselves. The United States would train a 70,000-member army. Japan would disarm some 100,000 militia fighters. Britain would mount an antinarcotics program. Italy would carry out changes in the judiciary. And Germany would train a 62,000-member police force.

But that meant no one was in overall command, officials now say. Many holes emerged in the American effort.

There were so few State Department or Pentagon civil affairs officials that 13 teams of C.I.A. operatives, whose main job was to hunt terrorists and the Taliban, were asked to stay in remote corners of Afghanistan to coordinate political efforts, said John E. McLaughlin, who was deputy director and then acting director of the agency. "It took us quite awhile to get them regrouped in the southeast for counterterrorism," he said of the C.I.A. teams.

Sixteen months after the president's 2002 speech, the United States Agency for International Development, the government's main foreign development arm, had seven full-time staffers and 35 full-time contract staff members in Afghanistan, most of them Afghans, according to a government audit. Sixty-one agency positions were vacant.

"It was state-building on the cheap, it was a duct tape approach," recalled Said T. Jawad, Mr. Karzai's chief of staff at the time and Afghanistan's current ambassador to Washington. "It was fixing things that were broken, not a strategic approach."

A SHIFT OF RESOURCES TO IRAQ

In October 2002, Robert Grenier, a former director of the C.I.A.'s counterintelligence center, visited the new Kuwait City headquarters of Lt. Gen David McKiernan, who was already planning the Iraq invasion. Meeting in a sheet metal warehouse, Mr. Grenier asked General McKiernan what his intelligence needs would be in Iraq. The answer was simple. "They wanted as much as they could get," Mr. Grenier said.

Throughout late 2002 and early 2003, Mr. Grenier said in an interview, "the best experienced, most qualified people who we had been using in Afghanistan shifted over to Iraq," including the agency's most skilled counterterrorism specialists and Middle East and paramilitary operatives.

That reduced the United States' influence over powerful Afghan warlords who were refusing to turn over to the central government tens of millions of dollars they had collected as customs payments at border crossings.

While the C.I.A. replaced officers shifted to Iraq, Mr. Grenier said, it did so with younger agents, who lacked the knowledge and influence of the veterans. "I think we could have done a lot more on the Afghan side if we had more experienced folks," he said.

A former senior official of the Pentagon's Central Command, which was running both wars, said that as the Iraq planning sped up, the military's covert Special Mission Units, like Delta Force and Navy Seals Team Six, shifted to Iraq from Afghanistan.

So did aerial surveillance "platforms" like the Predator, a remotely piloted spy plane armed with Hellfire missiles that had been effective at identifying targets in the mountains of Afghanistan. Predators were not shifted directly from Afghanistan to Iraq, according to the former official, but as new Predators were produced, they went to Iraq.

"We were economizing in Afghanistan," said the former official, who requested anonymity because he was not authorized to comment publicly. "The marginal return for one more platform in Afghanistan is so much greater than for one more in Iraq."

The shift in priorities became apparent to Dov Zakheim, the Pentagon's former comptroller, as planning for the Iraq war was in high gear in the fall of 2002. Mr. Rumsfeld asked him to serve as the Pentagon's reconstruction coordinator in Afghanistan. It was an odd role for the comptroller, whose primary task is managing the Pentagon's $400 billion a year budget.

"The fact that they went to the comptroller to do something like that was in part a function of their growing preoccupation with Iraq," said Mr. Zakheim, who left the administration in 2004. "They needed somebody, given that the top tier was covering Iraq."

In an interview, President Bush's national security adviser, Stephen J. Hadley, insisted that there was no diversion of resources from Afghanistan, and he cited recently declassified statistics to show that troop levels in Afghanistan rose at crucial moments — like the 2004 Afghan election — even after the Iraq war began.

But the former Central Command official said: "If we were not in Iraq, we would have double or triple the number of Predators across Afghanistan, looking for Taliban and peering into the tribal areas. We'd have the 'black' Special Forces you most need to conduct precision operations. We'd have more C.I.A."

"We're simply in a world of limited resources, and those resources are in Iraq," the former official added. "Anyone who tells you differently is blowing smoke."

A PIECEMEAL OPERATION

As White House officials put together plans in the spring of 2003 for

President Bush to land on the deck of the aircraft carrier Abraham Lincoln and declare the end of major combat operations in Iraq, the Pentagon decided to make a similar, if less dramatic, announcement for Afghanistan.

On May 1, hours before Mr. Bush stood beneath a "Mission Accomplished" banner, Mr. Rumsfeld appeared at a news conference with Mr. Karzai in Kabul's threadbare 19th-century presidential palace. "We clearly have moved from major combat activity to a period of stability and stabilization and reconstruction activities," he said. "The bulk of the country today is permissive, it's secure."

The Afghanistan announcement was largely lost in the spectacle of Mr. Bush's speech. But the predictions of stability proved no less detached from events on the ground.

Three weeks later, Afghan government workers who had not been paid for months held street demonstrations in Kabul. An exasperated Mr. Karzai publicly threatened to resign and announced that his government had run out of money because warlords were hoarding the customs revenues. "There is no money in the government treasury," Mr. Karzai said.

At the same time, the American-led training of a new Afghan Army was proving far more difficult than officials in Washington had expected. The new force, plagued by high desertion rates, had only 2,000 soldiers. The Germans' effort to train police officers was off to an even slower start, and the British-led counternarcotics effort was dwarfed by an explosion in the poppy crop. Already, small groups of Taliban fighters had slipped back over the border from Pakistan and killed aid workers, stalling reconstruction in the south.

A senior White House official said in a recent interview that in retrospect, putting different countries in charge of different operations was a mistake. "We piecemealed it," he said. "One of the problems is when everybody has a piece, everybody's piece is made third and fourth priority. Nobody's piece is first priority. Stuff didn't get done."

A month after his announcement in Kabul, Mr. Rumsfeld's aides presented a strategy to the White House aimed at weakening warlords and engaging in state-building in Afghanistan. In some ways, it was the approach Mr. Rumsfeld had rejected right after the invasion.

Pentagon officials said that Mr. Rumsfeld's views began to shift after a December 2002 briefing by Marin Strmecki, an Afghanistan expert at the Smith Richardson Foundation, who argued that Afghanistan was not ungovernable and that it could be turned into a moderate, Muslim force in the region.

Mr. Strmecki said that the United States needed to help Afghans create credible national institutions and that Pashtuns, Afghanistan's largest ethnic group and historically the Taliban's base of support, needed a more prominent role in the government. Mr. Rumsfeld, according to aides, was impressed by Mr. Strmecki's emphasis on training Afghans to run their own government and hired him.

Then another personnel change helped alter Afghanistan policy. Mr. Khalilzad, an Afghan-American who was a senior National Security Council official and a special envoy to Iraq exiles, was appointed ambassador to Afghanistan.

Mr. Khalilzad said he accepted the job after Mr. Bush promised to greatly expand resources in Afghanistan. "We had gotten the president to a significant increase," Mr. Khalilzad recalled.

A leading neo-conservative, Mr. Khalilzad could get Ms. Rice or — if need be — Mr. Bush on the phone. He had been a counselor to Mr. Rumsfeld and had worked for Dick Cheney when Mr. Cheney was the first President Bush's defense secretary. "Zal could get things done," said Lt. Gen. David W. Barno, a former American military commander in Afghanistan.

When Mr. Khalilzad arrived in Kabul on Thanksgiving 2003, he brought nearly $2 billion — twice the amount of the previous year — as well as a new military strategy and private experts to intensifying rebuilding.

They started a reconstruction plan dubbed "accelerating success" that involved the kind of nation-building once dismissed by the administration. General Barno expanded "Provincial Reconstruction Teams" to build schools, roads and wells and to win the "hearts and minds" of Afghans. The teams amounted to a much smaller version of the force that Mr. Powell had proposed 18 months earlier.

By January 2004, Afghanistan had reached a compromise on a new Afghan Constitution. With American backing, Mr. Karzai weakened several warlords. In October 2004, Mr. Karzai, who had been appointed president, was elected. At the same time, NATO countries steadily sent more troops to Afghanistan, and soon Mr. Rumsfeld, needing troops for Iraq, proposed that NATO take over security for all of Afghanistan.

By spring 2005, Afghanistan seemed to be moving toward the success Mr. Bush had promised. But then, fearing that Iraq was spinning out of control, the White House asked Mr. Khalilzad to become ambassador to Baghdad.

A LINGERING THREAT

Before departing Afghanistan, Mr. Khalilzad fought a final battle within the administration. It revealed divisions within the American government over Pakistan's role in aiding the Taliban, a delicate subject as the administration tried to coax Pakistan's president, Gen. Pervez Musharraf, to cooperate.

In an interview on Afghan television, Mr. Khalilzad noted that Pakistani journalists had recently interviewed a senior Taliban commander in Pakistan. He questioned Pakistan's claim that it did not know the whereabouts of senior Taliban commanders — a form of skepticism discouraged in Washington, where the administration's line had always been that General Musharraf was doing everything he could.

"If a TV station can get in touch with them, how can the intelligence service of a country, which has nuclear bombs, and a lot of security and military forces, not find them?" Mr. Khalilzad asked.

Pakistani officials publicly denounced Mr. Khalilzad's comments and denied that they were harboring Taliban leaders. But Mr. Khalilzad had also exposed the growing rift between American officials in Kabul and those in Islamabad.

Mr. Grenier said that when he was the C.I.A. station chief in Islamabad the issue of fugitive Taliban leaders was repeatedly raised with senior Pakistani intelligence officials in 2002. "The results were just not there," he recalled. "And it was quite clear to me that it wasn't just bad luck."

Pakistan had backed the Taliban throughout the 1990s as a counterweight to an alliance of northern Afghan commanders backed by India, Pakistan's bitter rival. Pakistani officials also distrusted Mr. Karzai.

Deciding that the Pakistanis would not act on the Taliban, Mr. Grenier said he had urged them to focus on arresting Qaeda members, who he said were far more of a threat to the United States.

"From our perspective at the time, the Taliban was a spent force," he said, adding, "We were very much focused on Al Qaeda and didn't want to distract the Pakistanis from that."

But Mr. Khalilzad, American military officials and others in the administration argued that the Taliban were crossing from Pakistan into Afghanistan and killing American troops and aid workers. "Colleagues in Washington at various levels did not recognize that there was the problem of sanctuary and that this was important," Mr. Khalilzad said.

But it was not until 2006, after ordering a study on Afghanistan's future, that Mr. Bush strenuously pressed General Musharraf on the Taliban. Later, Mr. Bush told his aides he worried that "old school ties" between Pakistani intelligence and the Taliban endured, despite the general's assurances. The Pakistanis, one senior American commander said, were "hedging their bets."

"They're not sure that we are staying," he added. "And if we are gone, the Taliban is their next best option" to remain influential in Afghanistan.

As 2005 ended, the Taliban leaders remained in hiding in Pakistan, waiting for an opportunity to cross the border. Soon, they would find one.

TO AFGHANS, A FICKLE EFFORT

In September 2005, NATO defense ministers gathered in Berlin to complete plans for NATO troops to take over security in Afghanistan's volatile south. It was the most ambitious "out of area" operations in NATO history, and across Europe, leaders worried about getting support from their countries. Then, American military officials dropped a bombshell.

The Pentagon, they said, was considering withdrawing up to 3,000 troops from Afghanistan, roughly 20 percent of total American forces.

NATO's secretary general, Jaap de Hoop Scheffer, said he had protested to Mr. Rumsfeld that a partial American withdrawal would discourage others from sending troops.

In the end, the planned troop reduction was abandoned, but chiefly because the American ground commander at the time, Lt. Gen. Karl W. Eikenberry, concluded that the Taliban were returning and that he needed to shift troops to the east to try to stop them. But the announcement had sent a signal of a wavering American commitment.

"The Afghan people still doubt our staying power," General Eikenberry said. "They have seen the world walk away from them before."

To sell their new missions at home, British, Dutch and Canadian officials portrayed deployments to Afghanistan as safe, and better than sending troops to Iraq. Germany and Italy prevented their forces from being sent on combat missions in volatile areas. Those regions were to be left to the Americans, Canadians, British and Dutch.

Three months after announcing the proposed troop withdrawal, the White House Office of Management and Budget cut aid to Afghanistan by a third.

Ms. Rice said that much of the money allocated to Afghanistan the previous year had not been spent. "There was an absorption problem," she said.

Mr. Neumann, then the ambassador, said he had argued against the decision.

Even so, American assistance to Afghanistan dropped by 38 percent, from $4.3 billion in fiscal 2005 to $3.1 billion in fiscal 2006, according to a study by the Congressional Research Service.

By February 2006, Mr. Neumann had come to the conclusion that the Taliban were planning a spring offensive, and he sent a cable to his superiors.

"I had a feeling that the view was too rosy in Washington," recalled Mr. Neumann, who retired from the State Department in June. "I was concerned."

Mr. Neumann's cable proved prophetic. In the spring of 2006, the Taliban carried out their largest offensive since 2001, attacking British, Canadian and Dutch troops in southern Afghanistan.

Hundreds of Taliban swarmed into the south, setting up checkpoints, assassinating officials and burning schools. Suicide bombings quintupled to 136. Roadside bombings doubled. All told, 191 American and NATO troops died in 2006, a 20 percent increase over the 2005 toll. For the first time, it became nearly as dangerous, statistically, to serve as an American in Afghanistan as in Iraq.

Mr. Neumann said that while suicide bombers came from Pakistan, most Taliban fighters in southern Afghanistan were Afghans. Captured insurgents said they had taken up arms because a local governor favored a rival tribe, corrupt officials provided no services or their families needed money.

After cutting assistance in 2006, the United States plans to provide $9 billion in aid to Afghanistan in 2007, twice the amount of any year since 2001.

Despite warnings about the Taliban's resurgence from Mr. Neumann, Mr. Khalilzad and military officials, Ms. Rice said, "there was no doubt that people were surprised that the Taliban was able to regroup and come back in a large, well-organized force."

DIVISIONS OVER STRATEGY

In July 2006, NATO formally took responsibility for security through-out Afghanistan. To Americans and Europeans, NATO is the vaunted alliance that won the cold war. To Afghans it is little more than a strange, new acronym. And NATO and the Americans are divided over strategy.

The disagreement is evident on the wall of the office of Gen. Dan K. McNeill, the commander of the 35,000 NATO forces in Afghanistan, where he keeps a chart that is a sea of yellow and red blocks. Each block shows the restrictions that national governments have placed on their forces under his command. Red blocks represent tasks a country will not do, like hunting Taliban or Qaeda leaders. Yellow blocks indicate missions they are willing to consider after asking their capitals for approval.

In Washington, officials lament that NATO nations are unwilling to take the kinds of risks and casualties necessary to confront the Taliban. Across Europe, officials complain the United States never focused on reconstruction, and they blame American forces for mounting air attacks on the Taliban that cause large civilian casualties, turning Afghans against the West.

The debate over how the 2001 victory in Afghanistan turned into the current struggle is well under way.

"Destroying the Al Qaeda sanctuary in Afghanistan was an extraordinary strategic accomplishment," said Robert D. Blackwill, who was in charge of both Afghanistan and Iraq policy at the National Security Council, "but where we find ourselves now may have been close to inevitable, whether the U.S. went into Iraq or not. We were going to face this long war in Afghanistan as long as we and the Afghan government couldn't bring serious economic reconstruction to the countryside, and eliminate the Taliban's safe havens in Pakistan."

But Henry A. Crumpton, a former C.I.A. officer who played a key role in ousting the Taliban and became the State Department's counterterrorism chief, said winning a war like the one in Afghanistan required

American personnel to "get in at a local level and respond to people's needs so that enemy forces cannot come in and take advantage."

"These are the fundamentals of counterinsurgency, and somehow we forgot them or never learned them," he added. He noted that "the United States has 11 carrier battle groups, but we still don't have expeditionary nonmilitary forces of the kind you need to win this sort of war."

"We're living in the past," he said.

Among some current and former officials, a consensus is emerging that a more consistent, forceful American effort could have helped to keep the Taliban and Al Qaeda's leadership from regrouping.

Gen. James L. Jones, a retired American officer and a former NATO supreme commander, said Iraq caused the United States to "take its eye off the ball" in Afghanistan. He warned that the consequences of failure "are just as serious in Afghanistan as they are in Iraq."

"Symbolically, it's more the epicenter of terrorism than Iraq," he said. "If we don't succeed in Afghanistan, you're sending a very clear message to the terrorist organizations that the U.S., the U.N. and the 37 countries with troops on the ground can be defeated."

CARLOTTA GALL CONTRIBUTED REPORTING.

Obama Adds Troops,
but Maps Exit Plan

BY SHERYL GAY STOLBERG AND HELENE COOPER | DEC. 1, 2009

WEST POINT, N.Y. — President Obama announced Tuesday that he would speed 30,000 additional troops to Afghanistan in coming months, but he vowed to start bringing American forces home in the middle of 2011, saying the United States could not afford and should not have to shoulder an open-ended commitment.

Promising that he could "bring this war to a successful conclusion," Mr. Obama set out a strategy that would seek to reverse Taliban gains in large parts of Afghanistan, better protect the Afghan people, increase the pressure on Afghanistan to build its own military capacity and a more effective government and step up attacks on Al Qaeda in Pakistan.

"America, we are passing through a time of great trial," Mr. Obama said. "And the message that we send in the midst of these storms must be clear: that our cause is just, our resolve unwavering."

The military escalation Mr. Obama described and defended in his speech to a national television audience and 4,000 cadets at the United States Military Academy here, the culmination of a review that lasted three months, could well prove to be the most consequential decision of Mr. Obama's presidency.

In his 33-minute address, he sought to convince an increasingly skeptical nation that the resurgence of the Taliban in Afghanistan and the continued existence of Al Qaeda across the border in Pakistan — what he called a "cancer" on the region — were direct threats to the United States, and that he could achieve the seemingly contradictory goals of expanding American involvement in the war even as he sought to bring it to a close.

The scene in the hall was striking and somber: row after row of cadets, in their blue-gray uniforms, listening intently to a strategy that could put many of them in harm's way. "If I did not think that the security of the United States and the safety of the American people were at stake in Afghanistan, I would gladly order every single one of our troops home tomorrow," Mr. Obama said. "So no, I do not make this decision lightly." He called on foreign allies to step up their commitment, declaring, "This is not just America's war."

He delivered a pointed message to Hamid Karzai, the president of Afghanistan, saying, "The days of providing a blank check are over."

Addressing critics who have likened Afghanistan to Vietnam, Mr. Obama called the comparison "a false reading of history." And he spoke directly to the American people about the tough road ahead.

"Let me be clear: none of this will be easy," Mr. Obama said. "The struggle against violent extremism will not be finished quickly, and it extends well beyond Afghanistan and Pakistan. It will be an enduring test of our free society, and our leadership in the world."

DOUG MILLS/THE NEW YORK TIMES

Spelling out his plans for Afghanistan, President Obama said he could "bring this war to a successful conclusion."

With the economy weak and the issue of jobs foremost on Americans' minds, the president conceded that the new strategy would carry an expensive price tag, which he put at an additional $30 billion in the first year.

Yet with some Democrats talking of a war surtax, Mr. Obama offered no details of how he intended to pay for his new policy, saying only that he was "committed to addressing these costs openly and honestly."

White House advisers said they expected the administration would do so in the coming weeks, as officials including Secretary of Defense Robert M. Gates and Secretary of State Hillary Rodham Clinton testify on Capitol Hill starting Wednesday.

The approach laid out by Mr. Obama — not so much a new strategy as a doubling down on the one he embraced earlier this year — incorporated the basic goals and came close to the force levels proposed in the counterinsurgency plan that Gen. Stanley A. McChrystal, the top military commander in Afghanistan, put forward in September.

In that report, General McChrystal said, in stark language, that unless significantly more troops were sent, the war in Afghanistan was likely to be lost.

But by including an explicit timetable to begin a withdrawal, Mr. Obama highlighted the seemingly conflicting pressures defining the debate over how to proceed: to do what is necessary to ensure that the region is not a launching pad for attacks on the United States and its allies, and to disengage militarily as quickly as possible.

Senior administration officials suggested, however, that any initial withdrawal starting in mid-2011 could be very limited, depending on the military situation at that point.

"The pace, the nature and the duration of that transition are to be determined down the road by the president based on the conditions on the ground," said Michèle A. Flournoy, under secretary of defense for policy.

The initial political reactions showed the crosscurrents facing the White House. Republicans applauded the buildup of troops but questioned the commitment to a timetable for bringing them home.

"Setting a draw-down date before this surge has even begun is a mistake, and it sends a mixed message to both our friends and our enemies regarding our long-term commitment to success," said Senator John Cornyn, Republican of Texas.

But among many Democrats, the response ranged from noncommittal to outright opposition.

"I see no good reason for us to send another 30,000 or more troops to Afghanistan when we have so many pressing issues — like our economy — to deal with in this country," said Representative Louise M. Slaughter, Democrat of New York.

Mr. Obama is calculating, administration officials said, that the explicit promise of a drawdown will impress upon the Afghan government that his commitment is not open-ended.

Mr. Obama was less clear publicly on how he planned to address the issue of Pakistan, which many administration officials say will prove to be a far more intractable problem in the long term than Afghanistan.

Administration officials said that Mr. Obama had signed off on a plan by the Central Intelligence Agency to expand C.I.A. activities in Pakistan. The plan calls for more strikes against militants by drone aircraft, sending additional spies to Pakistan and securing a White House commitment to bulk up the C.I.A.'s budget for operations inside the country.

The expanded operations could include drone strikes in the southern province of Baluchistan, where senior Afghan Taliban leaders are believed to be hiding, officials said.

The new Afghanistan strategy draws heavily on lessons learned from Mr. Bush's "surge" and strategy shift in Iraq in 2007, which Mr. Obama opposed.

In addition to the influx of troops and the training of the Afghan Army, administration officials said they were taking other lessons from the Iraq buildup, like empowering local security forces to stand up to Taliban militants in their communities and enhancing the training of national forces by embedding American troops with Afghan counterparts and later pairing American and Afghan units to fight side by side.

The 30,000 troops that Mr. Obama is sending are part of what one administration official characterized as a short-term, high-intensity effort to regain the initiative against the Taliban.

Administration officials said that they were hoping to get a commitment for an additional 5,000 to 8,000 troops from NATO allies — perhaps as early as Friday at a foreign ministers' meeting in Brussels — which would bring the number of additional troops in Afghanistan to close to the 40,000 that General McChrystal was seeking.

Mr. Obama is sending three of the four brigades requested by General McChrystal. The first Marines will begin arriving as early as Christmas, and all forces will be in place by May, a senior administration official said.

The 30,000 new American troops will focus on securing and protecting the country's top population centers, including Kabul, Khost and Kandahar, the Taliban's spiritual capital. Military officials said that two brigades would go south, with the third going to eastern Afghanistan.

Military officers said that they could maintain pressure on insurgents in remote regions by using surveillance drones and reports from people in the field to find pockets of Taliban fighters and to guide attacks, in particular by Special Operations forces.

The strategy also includes expanded economic development and reconciliation with less radical members of the Taliban.

In addition, Mr. Obama is making tougher demands on the Afghan government; he spent an hour on the phone Monday with Mr. Karzai, White House officials said, and pressed him on the need to combat the corruption and drug trafficking, which many Western officials say has fueled the resurgence of the Taliban.

During the conversation, Mr. Obama, described by one White House official as "very explicit," pressed Mr. Karzai on the need to take steps that would show progress. Mr. Obama congratulated Mr.

Karzai on setting up a corruption task force, but also pressed him on the need to make sure that officials appointed by the government are untainted by corruption.

SHERYL GAY STOLBERG REPORTED FROM WEST POINT, AND HELENE COOPER FROM WASHINGTON. REPORTING WAS CONTRIBUTED BY PETER BAKER, DAVID E. SANGER, MARK MAZZETTI, CARL HULSE AND MARK LANDLER FROM WASHINGTON, AND CARLOTTA GALL FROM KABUL, AFGHANISTAN.

Keeping a Promise to Afghans

OPINION | BY THE NEW YORK TIMES | JAN. 13, 2015

THE LEGACY OF America's war in Afghanistan, which nominally ended on New Year's Eve, will come into sharper focus in the coming decade. Historians will spend years figuring out what went right or wrong and which of Washington's programs will prove to be of lasting value.

There is one crucial piece of unfinished business that will speak volumes at the end of the day: whether the United States kept its promise to Afghan military interpreters who were offered the opportunity to resettle in America in recognition of the monumental risks they took.

Congress created special visa programs for Afghan and Iraqi military linguists starting in 2006. Early on, it was managed with callous disregard for its intended Afghan beneficiaries; only a fraction of the petitions submitted were approved. Secretary of State John Kerry has taken commendable steps over the past two years to streamline the review process and approve a higher percentage of cases. But the State Department remains hamstrung by a problem of its own making that only Congress can fix.

About 12,000 Afghan linguists have pending applications for the special visa. Under current law, however, the State Department has the authority to issue only 4,000 visas over the next two years. This logjam was entirely avoidable if only Washington bureaucrats had operated with greater dispatch. During some of the toughest years of the war, American officials in Kabul and Washington sat on, or rejected, the bulk of applications in the pipeline. In 2010 and 2011, for instance, only a few dozen Afghan linguists — an astonishingly small number — were allowed to immigrate.

At the time, some American officials in Kabul took the view that the program would worsen the country's brain drain and that enabling young, bilingual, educated Afghans to leave their homeland would send the wrong message about the state of a war that Washington portrayed with disingenuous optimism over the years. Many Afghan linguists actually received rejection letters that described them, indefensibly and without evidence, as suspected threats.

The sad result was more than 6,500 visa slots that Congress set aside for the early years of the program expired, leaving brave Afghans and their families in limbo. Many are living in hiding today, unable to return to their native provinces where the Taliban hold sway.

Fortunately, their plight came to the attention of American servicemen and servicewomen, who have lobbied their representatives in Congress seeking help. As the scope of the problem became clear to lawmakers, a remarkable if unlikely coalition from opposite ends of the political spectrum came together in an effort to undo a monumental wrong.

In the House, Representative Earl Blumenauer, an Oregon Democrat, and Representative Adam Kinzinger, a Republican from Illinois who is a former Air Force pilot, led the effort last year to extend the program and authorize the 4,000 visa slots currently available. In the Senate, John McCain, a Republican from Arizona, and Jeanne Shaheen, a Democrat from New Hampshire, championed the cause.

In an era of partisan acrimony and gridlock on Capitol Hill, their leadership on this issue has been inspirational. But much remains to be done. The White House will soon present to Congress a budget request that will almost certainly include provisions to create new visa slots for Afghan linguists. Lawmakers should ensure those are financed and approved either as part of the defense bill, if they actually manage to pass one this year, or through stand-alone legislation.

Failing to give all eligible and deserving applicants a fair shot at a new start in the United States would represent an abdication of a promise that helped persuade linguists to put their lives on the line. That would add a shameful chapter to the legacy of a war that has been grim enough for Afghans.

In Afghanistan's Unwinnable War, What's the Best Loss to Hope For?

BY MAX FISHER | FEB. 1, 2018

AFTER 16 YEARS of war in Afghanistan, experts have stopped asking what victory looks like and are beginning to consider the spectrum of possible defeats.

All options involve acknowledging the war as failed, American aims as largely unachievable and Afghanistan's future as only partly salvageable. Their advocates see glimmers of hope barely worth the stomach-turning trade-offs and slim odds of success.

"I don't think there is any serious analyst of the situation in Afghanistan who believes that the war is winnable," Laurel Miller, a political scientist at the RAND Corporation, said in a podcast last summer, after leaving her State Department stint as acting special representative for Afghanistan and Pakistan.

This may be why, even after thousands have died and over $100 billion has been spent, even after the past two weeks of shocking bloodshed in Kabul, few expect the United States to try anything other than the status quo.

It is a strategy, as Ms. Miller described it, to "prevent the defeat of the Afghan government and prevent military victory by the Taliban" for as long as possible.

Though far from the most promising option, it is the least humiliating. But sooner or later, the United States and Afghanistan will find themselves facing one of Afghanistan's endgames — whether by choice or not.

1. NATION-BUILDING, MINUS THE NATION

"I'll tell you what my best-case scenario would be," said Frances Z. Brown, an Afghanistan expert at the Carnegie Endowment for International Peace.

That, she said, would see the American-led coalition abandon its efforts to impose a centralized state and instead allow Afghans to build their own state from the bottom-up.

It would mean accepting a central government that acts more like a horse trader among local strongmen and warlords. American and allied troops would guarantee enough security to sustain the state. Afghans would figure out the rest for themselves.

Over time, ideally, Afghans might develop a functioning economy, then something like real democracy and, finally, peace and stability.

"But what we know from other cases is that this takes generations," Ms. Brown said. "So the 18-month time frames we've always had for Afghanistan are not realistic."

The perpetual occupation necessary for this to work might also doom it. Continued foreign aid incentivizes Afghan elites, who are already on the verge of splintering, to compete rather than come together.

This approach would involve tolerating the Taliban's presence in rural areas. And rolling crises would be built into this model, so Afghans would have to hope that they would somehow never derail the decades of progress needed before lasting change could take hold.

2. STARTING OVER

If Afghanistan were forced back to square one, it might, some scholars think, be able to rebuild itself from scratch.

After all, humanity lived for millenniums in something resembling low-grade anarchy. Modern nation-states grew out of that chaos only recently.

This would start with the effective collapse of the state and American withdrawal. Because the Taliban are too weak and unpopular to retake the country, as most analysts believe, Afghanistan would splinter.

Out of the ashes, local warlords and strongmen would rise up. Without the United States forcing them to take sides in an all-or-nothing war, they might eventually accommodate one another, and the Taliban. Their fiefs, once stable, could coalesce over years or decades into a fully realized state.

Research by Dipali Mukhopadhyay, a Columbia University political scientist, suggests that the warlords would gravitate toward the kind of state building that occurred in medieval Europe over centuries.

Jennifer Murtazashvili, a University of Pittsburgh political scientist who studies state building and failure, said the process might unfold more quickly and stably in Afghanistan. She has studied rural Afghan communities that outside the reach of the state, have begun reproducing the basic building blocks of one.

But hers is only a theory, untested in modern history.

3. THE SOMALIA MODEL

In a sign of how far hopes have fallen, the war-torn East African country of Somalia is increasingly being raised as worthy of emulation.

The Afghan government would retreat to major cities. Formally, it would switch to a federal system, as Somalia did in 2012. But power would effectively flow to whichever warlords and strongmen — potentially including the Taliban — rose up in the countryside.

This would, in theory, combine the first two models. The government could reconstitute itself as it mediated between local enclaves that would one day reintegrate with the state.

"This is the outcome we have de facto ended up with, but not in a peaceful sense," Ms. Murtazashvili said. The government is receding and the warlords are rising, but the two are in conflict.

The Somalia model would manage that process of disintegration, like crash-landing a plane rather than waiting for it to fall from the sky. It would leave communities to find their own peace with the Taliban, which some in remote parts of the country are already doing.

In Somalia itself, this model has found mixed success. Security has improved nationwide, but a devolving state has been left unable to root out extremists, who still carry out devastating attacks.

4. A PEACE THAT SATISFIES NO ONE

The paradox of peace deals is that while all sides benefit, each fears that it will not do as well as it could — or that its enemies might do too well. This gives each an incentive to block all but the perfect deal, a dynamic so pronounced in Afghanistan that in 16 years, talks have never advanced far enough to make clear what each side considers acceptable.

"I doubt the Taliban has even given any thought at a higher level to what a government looks like that it could have a stake in," said Courtney Cooper, a Council on Foreign Relations analyst.

The fear of losing out is not misplaced. Afghan elites already squabble over control of ministries and lucrative patronage networks, and their infighting grows as those resources shrink. In any peace deal, they would need to surrender many or most of those resources to the Taliban.

The Taliban, too, would probably need to surrender or curtail their hopes for dominating Afghanistan. That could anger the extremists rising in the group's ranks.

And any American president would risk a political backlash for appearing to usher the Taliban back into power. Veterans and military leaders might reasonably ask what they had fought for.

The clearest winner of any deal might be the Afghans themselves, but they are largely at the mercy of political actors for whom peace is risky.

5. A POST-AMERICAN CIVIL WAR

There is a more pessimistic version of the collapse-then-rebuild model, in which warlords compete until one prevails over all.

Afghanistan itself offers a particularly vivid example of this scenario: After the 1992 collapse of the Soviet-backed government there, the country was gripped by a terrible civil war. If the Americans abandoned the government now in place, that history could repeat.

"There is a strong possibility that this county could splinter, and not in consensual ways," Ms. Murtazashvili said.

That war culminated, in 1996, with one faction prevailing: the Taliban. It then sheltered Al Qaeda, prompting the American-led invasion and the war still raging all these years later.

That history, too, could repeat. Research by Barbara F. Walter, a political scientist at the University of California, San Diego, has found that extremists tend to prevail in civil war, and to do better as the war drags on. If the Americans exit Afghanistan, it might not be for long.

6. PERPETUAL STALEMATE

The likeliest outcome may be allowing the status quo to continue, even as all sides suffer under rising violence.

Neither the government nor the Taliban are strong enough to retake control. Outside actors like the United States and Pakistan may be unable to impose their vision of victory, but they can forestall losing indefinitely.

Foreign aid can sustain the government, even as its control of the country shrinks. There is little to stop the Taliban from carrying out ever more brazen attacks in the capital. The death toll, already high, would probably rise.

Eventually, the stalemate would almost certainly break, hurtling Afghanistan into one of its possible endgames. But it is difficult to say when.

"It's hard to think of an analogous case," said Ms. Brown, the Carnegie Afghanistan expert.

Few modern wars have raged this long, this destructively and with this much outside intervention. If there is an obvious way out, history does not provide it.

Drone Strikes Reveal Uncomfortable Truth: U.S. Is Often Unsure About Who Will Die

BY SCOTT SHANE | APRIL 23, 2015

BARACK OBAMA inherited two ugly, intractable wars in Iraq and Afghanistan when he became president and set to work to end them. But a third, more covert war he made his own, escalating drone strikes in Pakistan and expanding them to Yemen and Somalia.

The drone's vaunted capability for pinpoint killing appealed to a president intrigued by a new technology and determined to try to keep the United States out of new quagmires. Aides said Mr. Obama liked the idea of picking off dangerous terrorists a few at a time, without endangering American lives or risking the yearslong bloodshed of conventional war.

"Let's kill the people who are trying to kill us," he often told aides.

By most accounts, hundreds of dangerous militants have, indeed, been killed by drones, including some high-ranking Qaeda figures. But for six years, when the heavy cloak of secrecy has occasionally been breached, the results of some strikes have often turned out to be deeply troubling.

Every independent investigation of the strikes has found far more civilian casualties than administration officials admit. Gradually, it has become clear that when operators in Nevada fire missiles into remote tribal territories on the other side of the world, they often do not know who they are killing, but are making an imperfect best guess.

The president's announcement on Thursday that a January strike on Al Qaeda in Pakistan had killed two Western hostages, and that it took many weeks to confirm their deaths, bolstered the assessments of the program's harshest outside critics. The dark picture was compounded by the additional disclosure that two American members of

Al Qaeda were killed in strikes that same month, but neither had been identified in advance and deliberately targeted.

In all, it was a devastating acknowledgment for Mr. Obama, who had hoped to pioneer a new, more discriminating kind of warfare. Whether the episode might bring a long-delayed public reckoning about targeted killings, long hidden by classification rules, remained uncertain.

Even some former Obama administration security officials have expressed serious doubts about the wisdom of the program, given the ire it has ignited overseas and the terrorists who have said they plotted attacks because of drones. And outside experts have long called for a candid accounting of the results of strikes.

"I hope this event allows us at last to have an honest dialogue about the U.S. drone program," said Rachel Stohl, of the Stimson Center, a Washington research institute. "These are precise weapons. The failure is in the intelligence about who it is that we are killing."

Ms. Stohl noted that Mr. Obama and his top aides have repeatedly promised greater openness about the drone program but have never really delivered on it.

In a speech in 2013 about drones, Mr. Obama declared that no strike was taken without "near-certainty that no civilians will be killed or injured." He added that "nevertheless, it is a hard fact that U.S. strikes have resulted in civilian casualties" and said "those deaths will haunt us as long as we live."

But over the Obama presidency, it has become harder for journalists to obtain information from the government on the results of particular strikes. And Mr. Obama's Justice Department has fought in court for years to keep secret the legal opinions justifying strikes. Micah Zenko, a scholar at the Council on Foreign Relations and lead author of a 2013 study of drones, said the president's statement "highlights what we've sort of known: that most individuals killed are not on a kill list, and the government does not know their names."

Mr. Zenko noted that with the new disclosures, a total of eight Americans have been killed in drone strikes. Of those, only one, the

American cleric Anwar al-Awlaki, who joined Al Qaeda in Yemen and was killed in 2011, was identified and deliberately targeted. The rest were killed in strikes aimed at other militants, or in so-called signature strikes based on indications that people on the ground were likely with Al Qaeda or allied militant groups.

Though by most accounts six of the eight Americans were allied with Al Qaeda, Obama administration lawyers have ruled that a special legal review should be conducted before killing Americans suspected of terrorism. Such a review, they have argued, amounts to the legal "due process" required by the Constitution, though some legal scholars do not believe such reviews meet the constitutional test.

When Americans have been killed, however, the Obama administration has found it necessary to break with its usual practice and eventually acknowledge the deaths, at least in private discussions with reporters.

That was the case in the first C.I.A. drone strike, in Yemen in 2002, which turned out to have killed an American in Al Qaeda. It was the case in 2011, when an American Qaeda propagandist from North Carolina, Samir Khan, was killed along with Mr. Awlaki. And it happened two weeks later, when another American strike killed Mr. Awlaki's 16-year-old son and his 17-year-old cousin.

Military and intelligence officials said they did not know that the teenagers were present when they took a shot at a Qaeda operative who, it turned out, was not there. But such admissions, in the rare cases that officials were willing to discuss, undercut their argument that in most cases they were confident that they were killing only dangerous militants.

Most security experts still believe that drones, which allow a scene to be watched for hours or days through video feeds, still offer at least the chance of greater accuracy than other means of killing terrorists. By most accounts, conventional airstrikes and ground invasions kill a higher proportion of noncombatants. But without detailed, reliable, on-the-ground intelligence, experience has shown, drones make it possible to precisely kill the wrong people.

Mr. Zenko said that an average of separate counts of American drone strikes by three organizations, the New America Foundation, the Bureau of Investigative Journalism and The Long War Journal, finds that 522 strikes have killed 3,852 people, 476 of them civilians. But those counts, based on news accounts and some on-the-ground interviews, are considered very rough estimates.

The proliferating mistakes have given drones a sinister reputation in Pakistan and Yemen and have provoked a powerful anti-American backlash in the Muslim world. Part of the collateral damage in the strikes has been Mr. Obama's dream of restoring the United States' reputation with Muslims around the globe.

Despite the bad reviews overseas, drone strikes remain persistently popular with the American public, with about two-thirds expressing approval in polls. And despite the protests of a few liberal Democrats or libertarian Republicans, they have enjoyed unusual bipartisan support in Congress, where they are viewed as reducing the threat of terrorist attack and keeping American operators out of harm's way.

Mr. Zenko said that Mr. Obama and Congress should create a commission to examine the targeted killing program, its results and its flaws. But he said the combination of public and Congressional popularity probably means that even the latest disclosures will not bring such scrutiny to the program.

"I predict that even this episode will have no effect," he said.

MATT APUZZO AND MATTHEW ROSENBERG CONTRIBUTED REPORTING.

Telling the Truth
About the Cost of War

OPINION | BY THE NEW YORK TIMES | NOV. 23, 2017

A HALF-CENTURY AGO, the Pentagon's misleading claims about civilian deaths in Vietnam eroded public trust and, ultimately, support for the war. The United States military today claims to have learned the hard lessons of that and subsequent wars. It's put in place an elaborate system intended to minimize civilian casualties, including an Obama-era requirement that forces have "near certainty" that no civilian will be harmed before launching an attack. Intelligence analysts select targets, "targeteers" study models to calculate the most precise angles to strike, teams of lawyers evaluate plans and the Pentagon later discloses the few civilians who still, inevitably and tragically, wind up getting killed.

It turns out this is all, at least partly, an illusion. The Pentagon is killing far more civilians than it acknowledges, according to a recent report in The New York Times and other findings. A system intended to ensure transparency and accountability appears, instead, to be enabling the Pentagon to fool itself as well as the rest of us about the true cost of its strikes. It is often feeding bad intelligence into its intricate targeting system in the first place and then failing to thoroughly investigate civilians deaths after an attack.

The American-led military coalition has claimed, for instance, that the ratio of civilian deaths to airstrikes in the operation against the Islamic State in Iraq is one for every 157 strikes. The New York Times Sunday Magazine's account found a ratio of one civilian death for every five airstrikes — more than 31 times the Pentagon's claim. The true number, wrote the authors, Azmat Khan and Anand Gopal, "is at such a distance from official claims that, in terms of civilian deaths, this may be the least transparent war in recent American history."

Ms. Khan's and Mr. Gopal's reporting provided the first systematic, ground-based sample of airstrikes in Iraq since the operation

ANTOINE MAILLARD

began in 2014. They visited the sites of nearly 150 airstrikes in northern Iraq after ISIS was expelled, and they interviewed hundreds of witnesses, survivors and others. They photographed bomb fragments and mapped the destruction with satellite imagery, and they took the data to experts at the United States base in Qatar.

The article's organizing narrative was the tragic story of Bassim Razzo, whose wife, daughter, nephew and brother were killed in 2015 in coalition airstrikes on their side-by-side homes in Mosul, the main ISIS stronghold in Iraq. Video and written records showed that the coalition misidentified the two compounds as an ISIS car-bomb factory or command center. Before the writers took up the case, coalition officials had not included the Razzo family in its accounting of civilian victims. When Mr. Razzo asked for compensation, the military eventually offered the insulting sum of $15,000.

The Costs of War project at Brown University estimates over 200,000 civilians have been killed in Afghanistan, Iraq and Pakistan since 2001. Most experts attribute a majority of the civilian deaths to extremists.

Although international law obligates combatants to minimize harm to civilians, it is unrealistic to think that all civilian deaths can be prevented. Yet the reporting by Ms. Khan and Mr. Gopal suggests that America could be doing far more to protect civilians. They said they found a "consistent failure" by the American-led coalition to investigate claims carefully and to keep proper records. Some deaths occurred because civilians were close to ISIS targets. Many others, however, appear to have been recorded wrongly by "flawed or outdated intelligence that conflated civilians with combatants." The article said the military seldom recognized its failures or made changes to prevent civilian deaths.

To some extent, the American people may be blind to this carnage, having been lulled by their military and political leaders into believing that advanced technology and precision strikes kill the bad guys while sparing the innocent. This seductive concept took hold with video of seemingly pinpoint strikes during the first Persian Gulf war and was reinforced since by widespread use of drone strikes by Presidents George W. Bush, Barack Obama and Donald Trump against faraway targets.

However precise the weapons, careful the planners and skilled the fighters, war inevitably includes mistakes that kill civilians. Leaders need to be honest that there is no such thing as antiseptic combat, while Americans need to understand the full cost and consequences of military actions undertaken in their names.

These are not idle concerns. The pace of attacks and civilian casualties seems to be rising, and with them the potential for alienating the very people America hopes to save. The anti-ISIS fight has quickened and moved into crowded cities, but the president has also given field commanders more authority to make battlefield decisions in an ill-defined hunt for terrorists.

Civilian deaths impose another penalty. They become a recruiting tool for terrorists and undermine counterterrorism operations. It's up to Congress to ensure true accountability and transparency, if the administration does not, by holding hearings and demanding answers.

Our Drone War Burnout

OPINION | BY PRATAP CHATTERJEE | JULY 14, 2015

SAN FRANCISCO — A man bleeds profusely from a leg shattered by a missile. He drags himself slowly across a field until he dies in the dirt. These images from Heather Linebaugh's dreams play back endlessly, even in her waking hours.

Cian Westmoreland dreams of dozens of children staring at the sky in terror. And Brandon Bryant writes poems about soldiers dying in a sea of blood, their bodies imagined in the grainy infrared imagery of military operations.

I interviewed all three young Air Force veterans in order to gain a greater understanding of the costs of the White House's secretive drone operations. As public support for foreign wars has fallen, following yearslong occupations of Afghanistan and Iraq, the Obama administration has favored this form of remote-control warfare. In the president's first five years in office, the C.I.A. made 330 drone strikes in Pakistan alone, compared with 51 strikes in four years of George W. Bush's presidency.

The rationale for weaponized drones was twofold. The powerful technology of high-quality video streamed in real time via satellite promised the capability to kill enemy combatants with pinpoint accuracy. At the same time, operations could be conducted in air-conditioned comfort in locations like the Nevada desert, keeping American personnel out of harm's way.

Neither assumption was correct.

The issue of drones' civilian body count is well documented. The C.I.A., in classified submissions to Congress, claims civilian death rates "typically in the single digits" per year, according to Senator Dianne Feinstein in 2013, who then chaired the Senate Intelligence Committee.

Independent sources differ sharply from the official account. In 646 probable drone strikes in Pakistan, Somalia and Yemen recorded by

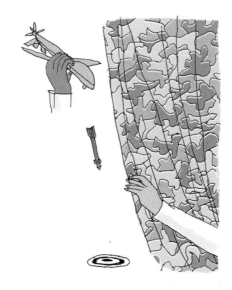

the Bureau of Investigative Journalism, as many as 1,128 civilians, including 225 children, were killed — 22 percent of deaths. The New America Foundation's estimates are lower, but suggest a civilian death rate of about 10 percent.

The drone wars are also taking a toll at home. Air Force psychological studies have found widespread stress among pilots, analysts and operators.

"What we see are elevated rates of emotional exhaustion and distress," said Dr. Wayne Chappelle at the School of Aerospace Medicine at Wright-Patterson Air Force Base in Ohio.

The Air Force recently announced that only about 180 drone pilots graduate from training each year, while some 240 of the 1,260 pilots currently working expected not to continue once their six-year contracts expire. Soon after the Government Accountability Office discovered that only about one-third of drone pilots in a sample had completed their full training before being pressed into service, the Pentagon reluctantly cut back on combat air patrols until it could find more pilots.

Pilots are only part of the story. As many as 180 people, from military lawyers and commanders to private contractors from Raytheon and Northrop Grumman, are required to maintain each patrol of three to four Predator or Reaper drones around the clock. Many technicians who review footage and other data are employed soon after high school, with less than a year of training.

None of the veterans mentioned earlier ever came close to an actual battlefield. Mr. Westmoreland worked at a military base in Kandahar, Afghanistan, where he helped set up a relay system to beam aerial footage to Al Udeid Air Base in Qatar. Mr. Bryant managed cameras on a Predator drone from Nellis Air Force Base, Nevada. Ms. Linebaugh's job was analyzing video feeds at Beale Air Force Base in California.

Yet they all attest to the stress and psychological impacts of their work. Working up to 12 hours a day, sometimes six days a week, analysts watch their targets up close for months on end. They often witness their subjects' final moments. In follow-up surveillance, they may even view their funerals.

"Watching targets go about their daily lives may inspire empathy," said Julie Carpenter, a research fellow at California Polytechnic State University who has studied human-technology interactions in the military. The Air Force is providing psychological support for drone personnel, but this interim solution seems unlikely to be adequate.

"We can say we see children and we think you shouldn't do it. But it isn't up to us," one former analyst, who asked to remain anonymous, told me. "We are completely outranked, and at the very bottom of the food chain."

Stories of the psychological trauma suffered by lower-ranked Air Force personnel are starting to emerge. Veterans like Mr. Bryant, Ms. Linebaugh and Mr. Westmoreland have attested in documentaries and the media to deep-seated flaws they've observed in drone warfare.

We need far greater transparency about the targeted killing operations. From the glimpses we have seen, we know there have been tragic failures. In 2011, a transcript of a drone strike, obtained under the Freedom of Information Act by The Los Angeles Times, revealed widespread confusion among imagery analysts in Florida, pilots in Nevada and the missile operators on Kiowa helicopters in Afghanistan, resulting in the killing of some two dozen innocent civilians with no terrorist connections.

In 1971, in the wake of the My Lai Vietnam massacre, Vietnam Veterans Against the War held a series of hearings in Detroit called the Winter Soldier Investigation. The purpose was not to scapegoat anyone, but to gather testimony on military policies and war crimes from those who experienced the atrocity firsthand.

We need a similar forum today. For a full accounting of the impact of America's drone wars, at home and abroad, our representatives in Congress must hear directly from the veterans.

PRATAP CHATTERJEE IS THE EXECUTIVE DIRECTOR OF CORPWATCH, AN INVESTIGATIVE JOURNALISM GROUP, AND THE CO-AUTHOR OF THE FORTHCOMING GRAPHIC NOVEL "VERAX."

I Helped Sell the False Choice of War Once. It's Happening Again.

OPINION | BY LAWRENCE WILKERSON | FEB. 5, 2018

FIFTEEN YEARS AGO this week, Colin Powell, then the secretary of state, spoke at the United Nations to sell pre-emptive war with Iraq. As his chief of staff, I helped Secretary Powell paint a clear picture that war was the only choice, that when "we confront a regime that harbors ambitions for regional domination, hides weapons of mass destruction and provides haven and active support for terrorists, we are not confronting the past, we are confronting the present. And unless we act, we are confronting an even more frightening future."

Following Mr. Powell's presentation on that cold day, I considered what we had done. At the moment, I thought all our work was for naught — and despite his efforts we did not gain substantial international buy-in. But polls later that day and week demonstrated he did convince many Americans. I knew that was why he was chosen to make the presentation in the first place: his standing with the American people was more solid than that of any other member of the Bush administration.

President George W. Bush would have ordered the war even without the United Nations presentation, or if Secretary Powell had failed miserably in giving it. But the secretary's gravitas was a significant part of the two-year-long effort by the Bush administration to get Americans on the war wagon.

That effort led to a war of choice with Iraq — one that resulted in catastrophic losses for the region and the United States-led coalition, and that destabilized the entire Middle East.

This should not be forgotten, since the Trump administration is using much the same playbook to create a false impression that war is the only way to address the threats posed by Iran.

Just over a month ago, the United States ambassador to the United Nations, Nikki Haley, said that the administration had "undeniable" evidence that Iran was not complying with Security Council resolutions regarding its ballistic missile program and Yemen. Just like Mr. Powell, Ms. Haley showed satellite images and other physical evidence available only to the United States intelligence community to prove her case. But the evidence fell significantly short.

It's astonishing how similar that moment was to Mr. Powell's 2003 presentation on Iraq's weapons of mass destruction — and how the Trump administration's methods overall match those of President Bush and Vice President Dick Cheney. As I watched Ms. Haley at the Defense Intelligence Agency, I wanted to play the video of Mr. Powell on the wall behind her, so that Americans could recognize instantly how they were being driven down the same path as in 2003 — ultimately to war. Only this war with Iran, a country of almost 80 million people whose vast strategic depth and difficult terrain make it a far greater challenge than Iraq, would be 10 to 15 times worse than the Iraq war in terms of casualties and costs.

If we want a slightly more official statement of the Trump administration's plans for Iran, we need only look at the recently released National Security Strategy, which says, "The longer we ignore threats from countries determined to proliferate and develop weapons of mass destruction, the worse such threats become, and the fewer defensive options we have." The Bush-Cheney team could not have said it better as it contemplated invading Iraq.

The strategy positions Iran as one of the greatest threats America faces, much the same way President Bush framed Saddam Hussein's Iraq. With China, Russia and North Korea all presenting vastly more formidable challenges to America and its allies than Iran, one has to wonder where the Trump team gets its ideas.

Though Ms. Haley's presentation missed the mark, and no one other than the national security elite will even read the strategy, it won't matter. We've seen this before: a campaign built on the politicization of intelligence and shortsighted policy decisions to make the case for war. And the American people have apparently become so accustomed to executive branch warmongering — approved almost unanimously by the Congress — that such actions are not significantly contested.

So far, news organizations have largely failed to refute false narratives coming out of the Trump White House on Iran. In early November, news outlets latched onto claims by unnamed American officials that newly released documents from Osama bin Laden's compound represented "evidence of Iran's support of Al Qaeda's war with the United States."

It's a vivid reminder of Vice President Cheney's desperate attempts in 2002-03 to conjure up evidence of Saddam Hussein's relationship with Al Qaeda from detainees at Guantánamo Bay. It harks back to the C.I.A. director George Tenet's assurances to Mr. Powell that the connection between Saddam Hussein and Osama bin Laden was ironclad in the lead-up to his United Nations presentation. Today, we know how terribly wrong Mr. Tenet was.

Today, the analysts claiming close ties between Al Qaeda and Iran come from the Foundation for Defense of Democracies, which vehemently opposes the Iran nuclear deal and unabashedly calls for regime change in Iran.

It seems not to matter that 15 of the 19 hijackers on Sept. 11 were Saudis and none were Iranians. Or that, according to the United States intelligence community, of the groups listed as actively hostile to the United States, only one is loosely affiliated with Iran, and Hezbollah doesn't make the cut. More than ever the Foundation for Defense of Democracies seems like the Pentagon's Office of Special Plans that pushed falsehoods in support of waging war with Iraq.

The Trump administration's case for war with Iran ranges much wider than Ms. Haley's work. We should include the president's decertification ultimatum in January that Congress must "fix" the Iran nuclear deal, despite the reality of Iran's compliance; the White House's pressure on the intelligence community to cook up evidence of Iran's noncompliance; and the administration's choosing to view the recent protests in Iran as the beginning of regime change. Like the Bush administration before, these seemingly disconnected events serve to create a narrative in which war with Iran is the only viable policy.

As I look back at our lock-step march toward war with Iraq, I realize that it didn't seem to matter to us that we used shoddy or cherry-picked intelligence; that it was unrealistic to argue that the war would "pay for itself," rather than cost trillions of dollars; that we might be hopelessly naïve in thinking that the war would lead to democracy instead of pushing the region into a downward spiral.

The sole purpose of our actions was to sell the American people on the case for war with Iraq. Polls show that we did. Mr. Trump and his team are trying to do it again. If we're not careful, they'll succeed.

LAWRENCE WILKERSON, A RETIRED ARMY COLONEL WHO TEACHES AT THE COLLEGE OF WILLIAM & MARY, WAS CHIEF OF STAFF TO SECRETARY OF STATE COLIN POWELL FROM 2002 TO 2005.

Glossary

Al Qaeda A radical terrorist organization founded by Osama bin Laden that is opposed to Western foreign policy.

Allied powers The countries including Great Britain, the Soviet Union, China, France and the United States that opposed the Axis powers during World War II.

Axis powers The countries including Nazi Germany, Italy and Japan that opposed the Allied powers during World War II.

civil war A war between opposing citizens of the same country.

counter-insurgency Military action taken against the activities of guerrillas or rebels.

despotism A political system in which the leader holds absolute power, often in an oppressive way.

drone strike A military operation carried out by a remote-controlled unmanned aircraft.

guerrilla A member of an independent group carrying out irregular fighting against larger government forces.

insurgency An active revolt or uprising against a government that is less organized than a rebellion.

neutrality The state of not supporting either side in a conflict or war.

Pentagon The building in Washington, D.C. that serves as the head-quarters of the United States Department of Defense.

sectarian violence A form of violence between different sects or groups within a particular ideology or religion.

stalemate A situation in which no action or progress can be made; a form of deadlock.

Taliban An Islamic fundamentalist group based in Afghanistan.

terrorism The systematic use of terror as a means of coercion; the use of violence against civilians to pursue political aims.

trench warfare A form of battle in which opposing forces attack one another from trenches dug into the ground. Primarily used during World War I.

U-boat German submarines used in World War I and World War II.

Vietcong A member of the Communist guerrilla forces in North Vietnam that fought the South Vietnamese and the United States troops in the Vietnam War.

weapon of mass destruction (WMD) A chemical, biological, or nuclear weapon capable of a high order of destruction or causing mass casualties.

Media Literacy Terms

"Media literacy" refers to the ability to access, understand, critically assess and create media. The following terms are important components of media literacy, and they will help you critically engage with the articles in this title.

angle The aspect of a news story that a journalist focuses on and develops.

attribution The method by which a source is identified or by which facts and information are assigned to the person who provided them.

balance Principle of journalism that both perspectives of an argument should be presented in a fair way.

bias A disposition of prejudice in favor of a certain idea, person or perspective.

byline Name of the writer, usually placed between the headline and the story.

caption Identifying copy for a picture; also called a legend or cutline.

commentary Type of story that is an expression of opinion on recent events by a journalist generally known as a commentator.

credibility The quality of being trustworthy and believable, said of a journalistic source.

editorial Article of opinion or interpretation.

human interest story Type of story that focuses on individuals and how events or issues affect their lives, generally offering a sense of relatability to the reader.

impartiality Principle of journalism that a story should not reflect a journalist's bias and should contain balance.

intention The motive or reason behind something, such as the publication of a news story.

motive The reason behind something, such as the publication of a news story or a source's perspective on an issue.

news story An article or style of expository writing that reports news, generally in a straightforward fashion and without editorial comment.

op-ed An opinion piece that reflects a prominent writer's opinion on a topic of interest.

paraphrase The summary of an individual's words, with attribution, rather than a direct quotation of their exact words.

quotation The use of an individual's exact words indicated by the use of quotation marks and proper attribution.

reliability The quality of being dependable and accurate, said of a journalistic source.

source The origin of the information reported in journalism.

style A distinctive use of language in writing or speech; also a news or publishing organization's rules for consistent use of language with regards to spelling, punctuation, typography and capitalization, usually regimented by a house style guide.

Media Literacy Questions

1. Identify the various sources cited in the article "3,000 Deaths in Iraq, Countless Tears at Home" (on page 129). How do the journalists attribute information to each of these sources in their article? How effective are their attributions in helping the reader identify their sources?

2. In "How a 'Good War' in Afghanistan Went Bad" (on page 166), David Rohde and David E. Sanger paraphrase information from Donald Rumsfeld. What are the strengths of the use of a paraphrase as opposed to a direct quote? What are its weaknesses?

3. Compare the headlines of "The War to End All Wars? Hardly. But It Did Change Them Forever." (on page 31) and "Telling the Truth About the Cost of War" (on page 200). Which is a more compelling headline, and why? How could the less compelling headline be changed to better draw the reader's interest?

4. What type of story is "End of a Nightmare" (on page 74)? Can you identify another article in this collection that is the same type of story?

5. Does John Tagliabue demonstrate the journalistic principle of balance in his article "Wave of Protests, From Europe to New York" (on page 101)? If so, how did he do so? If not, what could he have included to make his article more balanced?

6. The article "Fifteen Years Ago, America Destroyed My Country" (on page 144) is an example of an op-ed. Identify how Sinan Antoon's attitude, tone and bias help convey his opinion on the topic.

7. Does "U.S. and Britain Strike Afghanistan, Aiming at Bases and Terrorist Camps; Bush Warns 'Taliban Will Pay a Price' " (on page 152) use multiple sources? What are the strengths of using multiple sources in a journalistic piece? What are the weaknesses of relying heavily on few sources?

8. "Drone Strikes Reveal Uncomfortable Truth: U.S. Is Often Unsure About Who Will Die" (on page 196) features a chart. What does this chart add to the article?

9. Often, as a news story develops, journalists' attitudes toward the subject may change. Compare "Obama Adds Troops, but Maps Exit Plan" (on page 183) and "Obama Declares an End to Combat Mission in Iraq" (on page 139), both by Helene Cooper and Sheryl Gay Stolberg. Did new information discovered between the publication of these two articles change Stolberg and Cooper's perspective?

10. Analyze Nicholas Kristof's perspective in the op-ed piece "A Merciful War" (on page 163). What evidence does Kristof use to support his perspective? In what way is the evidence effective or ineffective?

11. What is the intention of the article "Voice of Verdun: France's Reply to Peace Hints" (on page 13)? How effectively does it achieve its intended purpose?

12. Identify each of the sources in "What Was the Vietnam War About?" (on page 77) as a primary source or a secondary source. Evaluate the reliability and credibility of each source. How does your evaluation of each source change your perspective on this article?

Citations

All citations in this list are formatted according to the
Modern Language Association's (MLA) style guide.

BOOK CITATION

NEW YORK TIMES EDITORIAL STAFF, THE. *War*. New York: New York Times
   Educational Publishing, 2019.

ARTICLE CITATIONS

ALVAREZ, LIZETTE, AND ANDREW LEHREN. "3,000 Deaths in Iraq, Countless
   Tears at Home." *The New York Times*, 1 Jan. 2007, https://www.nytimes
   .com/2007/01/01/us/01deaths.html.

ANTOON, SINAN. "Fifteen Years Ago, America Destroyed My Country." *The New
   York Times*, 18 Mar. 2018, https://www.nytimes.com/2018/03/19/opinion/
   iraq-war-anniversary-.html.

APPY, CHRISTIAN G. "What Was the Vietnam War About?" *The New York Times*,
   26 Mar. 2018, https://www.nytimes.com/2018/03/26/opinion/what was the
   -vietnam-war-about.html.

BALDWIN, HANSON W. "War of the World: Japanese Attack Merges Conflicts—
   We Must Not Discount Foe's Strength." *The New York Times*, 8 Dec. 1941,
   https://www.nytimes.com/1941/12/08/archives/-japanese-attack-merges
   -conflicts-we-must-not-discount-foes.html.

BURNS, JOHN F. "Cheers, Tears and Looting in Capital's Streets." *The New York
   Times*, 10 Apr. 2003, https://www.nytimes.com/2003/04/10/world/a-nation
   -at-war-tumult-cheers-tears-and-looting-in-capital-s-streets.html.

CHATTERJEE, PRATAP. "Our Drone War Burnout." *The New York Times*, 14 July 2015,
   https://www.nytimes.com/2015/07/14/opinion/our-drone-war-burnout.html.

COOPER, HELENE, AND SHERYL GAY STOLBERG. "Obama Declares an End to
   Combat Mission in Iraq." *The New York Times*, 31 Aug. 2010, https://www
   .nytimes.com/2010/09/01/world/01military.html?ref=middleeast.

ERLANGER, STEVEN. "The War to End All Wars? Hardly. But It Did Change Them Forever." *The New York Times*, 26 June 2014, https://www.nytimes.com/2014/06/27/world/europe/world-war-i-brought-fundamental-changes-to-the-world.html.

FISHER, MAX. "In Afghanistan's Unwinnable War, What's the Best Loss to Hope For?" *The New York Times*, 1 Feb. 2018, https://www.nytimes.com/2018/02/01/world/asia/afghanistan-war.html.

GAY STOLBERG, SHERYL, AND HELENE COOPER. "Obama Adds Troops, but Maps Exit Plan." *The New York Times*, 1 Dec. 2009, https://www.nytimes.com/2009/12/02/world/asia/02prexy.html.

KAZIN, MICHAEL. "Should America Have Entered World War I?" *The New York Times*, 6 Apr. 2017, https://www.nytimes.com/2017/04/06/opinion/should-america-have-entered-world-war-i.html.

KRISTOF, NICHOLAS D. "A Merciful War." *The New York Times*, 1 Feb. 2002, https://www.nytimes.com/2002/02/01/opinion/a-merciful-war.html.

LANGGUTH, JACK. "160 U.S. and Saigon Planes Bomb 2 Bases in North in Record Raid." *The New York Times*, 3 Mar. 1965, https://timesmachine.nytimes.com/timesmachine/1965/03/03/101530178.html.

MACKENZIE, CAMERON. "German Counter-Artillery Fire Silenced by Our Guns in 38 Minutes." *The New York Times,* 13 Sept. 1918, https://timesmachine.nytimes.com/timesmachine/1918/09/13/97028228.html.

MAZZETTI, MARK. "A Shifting Enemy: U.S. Generals Say Civil War, Not Insurgency, Is Greatest Threat." *The New York Times*, 18 Nov. 2006, https://www.nytimes.com/2006/11/18/world/middleeast/18military.html.

MEACHAM, JON. "Which Date Should Live in Infamy?" *The New York Times*, 10 Dec. 2016, https://www.nytimes.com/2016/12/10/opinion/sunday/which-date-should-live-in-infamy.html.

MYERS, STEVEN LEE, AND ALAN COWELL. "Long War Is Seen." *The New York Times*, 12 Oct. 2001, https://www.nytimes.com/2001/10/12/world/a-nation-challenged-the-military-long-war-is-seen.html.

THE NEW YORK TIMES. "All the Powers Massing Great Armies in Fear of Possible Conflict." *The New York Times,* 30 Jul. 2014, https://timesmachine.nytimes.com/timesmachine/1914/07/30/119124505.html.

THE NEW YORK TIMES. "The Americans Depart." *The New York Times*, 30 April 1975, https://www.timesmachine.nytimes.com/timesmachine/1975/04/30/76359486.html.

THE NEW YORK TIMES. "End of a Nightmare." *The New York Times*, 24 Jan.

1973, https://timesmachine.nytimes.com/timesmachine/1973/01/24/79834722.html.

THE NEW YORK TIMES. "Enemy Maneuvers." *The New York Times*, 7 May 1945, https://timesmachine.nytimes.com/timesmachine/1945/05/07/88224877.html.

THE NEW YORK TIMES. "The Failure to Find Iraqi Weapons." *The New York Times,* 26 Sept. 2003, https://www.nytimes.com/2003/09/26/opinion/the-failure-to-find-iraqi-weapons.html.

THE NEW YORK TIMES. "For Those Who Died." *The New York Times*, 7 May 1945, https://timesmachine.nytimes.com/timesmachine/1945/05/07/88224878.html.

THE NEW YORK TIMES. "Keeping a Promise to Afghans." *The New York Times,* 13 Jan. 2015, https://www.nytimes.com/2015/01/13/opinion/keeping-a-promise-to-afghans.html.

THE NEW YORK TIMES. "McNamara Report to Johnson on the Situation in Saigon in '63." *The New York Times*, 13 June 1971, https://timesmachine.nytimes.com/timesmachine/1971/06/13/170504922.html.

THE NEW YORK TIMES. "Telling the Truth About the Cost of War." *The New York Times,* 23 Nov. 2017, https://www.nytimes.com/2017/11/23/opinion/america-war-casualties-soldiers.html.

THE NEW YORK TIMES. "The War Begins." *The New York Times*, 20 Mar. 2003, https://www.nytimes.com/2003/03/20/opinion/the-war-begins.html.

THE NEW YORK TIMES. "Wilson Approves Staff's Army Bill." *The New York Times*, 7 Apr. 1917, https://timesmachine.nytimes.com/timesmachine/1917/04/07/102329717.html.

PEARSON, ANDREW. "How Vietnam Changed Journalism." *The New York Times,* 29 Mar. 2018, https://www.nytimes.com/2018/03/29/opinion/vietnam-war-journalism.html.

PERRIS, G.H. "Voice of Verdun France's Reply to Peace Hints." *The New York Times*, 18 Dec. 1916, https://www.nytimes.com/1916/12/18/archives/voice-of-verdun-frances-reply-to-peace-hints-victory-on-meuse-held.html.

ROHDE, DAVID, AND DAVID E. SANGER. "How a 'Good War' in Afghanistan Went Bad." *The New York Times*, 12 Aug. 2007, https://www.nytimes.com/2007/08/12/world/asia/12afghan.html.

SANGER, DAVID E., AND JOHN F. BURNS. "Bush Orders Start of War on Iraq; Missiles Apparently Miss Hussein." *The New York Times,* 20 Mar. 2003, https://www.nytimes.com/2003/03/20/world/threats-responses-white-house-bush-orders-start-war-iraq-missiles-apparently.html.

SANGER, DAVID E. "President Says Military Phase in Iraq Has Ended." *The New York Times*, 2 May 2003, https://www.nytimes.com/2003/05/02/international/worldspecial/president-says-military-phase-in-iraq-has-ended.html.

SHALETT, SIDNEY. "First Atomic Bomb Dropped on Japan; Missile Is Equal to 20,000 Tons of TNT; Truman Warns Foe of a 'Rain of Ruin'." *The New York Times*, 6 Aug. 1945, https://www.archive.nytimes.com/www.nytimes.com/learning/general/onthisday/big/0806.html.

SHANE, SCOTT. "Drone Strikes Reveal Uncomfortable Truth: U.S. Is Often Unsure About Who Will Die." *The New York Times*, 23 Apr. 2015, https://www.nytimes.com/2015/04/24/world/asia/drone-strikes-reveal-uncomfortable-truth-us-is-often-unsure-about-who-will-die.html.

SMALE, ALISON. "At the Site of Germany's Biggest World War II Battle, a Changing View of History." *The New York Times*, 18 July 2017, https://www.nytimes.com/2017/07/18/world/europe/seelow-heights-world-war-ii-germany-soviet-union.html.

TAGLIABUE, JOHN. "Wave of Protests, From Europe to New York." *The New York Times*, 21 Mar. 2003, https://www.nytimes.com/2003/03/21/world/a-nation-at-war-world-reaction-wave-of-protests-from-europe-to-new-york.html.

TYLER, PATRICK E. "U.S. and Britain Strike Afghanistan, Aiming at Bases and Terrorist Camps; Bush Warns 'Taliban Will Pay a Price'." *The New York Times*, 8 Oct. 2001, https://www.nytimes.com/2001/10/08/world/nation-challenged-attack-us-britain-strike-afghanistan-aiming-bases-terrorist.html.

UFFORD, MATT. "15 Years Ago, I Helped Start a War That Hasn't Ended." *The New York Times*, 20 Mar. 2018, https://www.nytimes.com/2018/03/20/magazine/iraq-war-invasion-15-years.html.

UPDEGROVE, MARK K. "Lyndon Johnson's Vietnam." *The New York Times*, 24 Feb. 2017, https://www.nytimes.com/2017/02/24/opinion/lyndon-johnsons-vietnam.html.

WIDMER, TED. "Long Echoes of War and Speech." *The New York Times*, 13 Aug. 2014, https://www.nytimes.com/2014/08/14/opinion/woodrow-wilson-world-war-1-and-american-idealism.html.

WILKERSON, LAWRENCE. "I Helped Sell the False Choice of War Once. It's Happening Again." *The New York Times*, 5 Feb. 2018, https://www.nytimes.com/2018/02/05/opinion/trump-iran-war.html.

WONG, EDWARD. "A Matter of Definition: What Makes a Civil War, and Who Declares It So?" *The New York Times*, 26 Nov. 2005, www.nytimes.com/2006/11/26/world/middleeast/26war.html.

Index